BEHAVIOURAL TREATMENTS
WITH CHILDREN

ROGER MORGAN BA(Wales), PhD(Leicester)

Deputy Director of Social Services
Oxfordshire

William Heinemann Medical Books Ltd
London

To Helen

Published by William Heinemann Medical Books Ltd
23 Bedford Square, London WC1B 3HH

First published 1984

© Roger Morgan 1984

ISBN: 0–433–22221–2

Phototypeset by Inforum Ltd, Portsmouth and
printed in Great Britain by
Biddles Ltd, Guildford, Surrey.

Contents

Acknowledgements

The cases in this book are based upon the treatments of numerous children in the different parts of the country where I have worked as a behaviour therapist. I am deeply indebted to my child patients, and to the parents and professional colleagues involved with me in their treatment.

I owe an especial debt of gratitude to Dr Gordon Young, who first introduced me to behaviour therapy and taught me to treat my first patients, and to Dr Keith Turner, Professor Derek Jehu and Professor Martin Herbert, who taught me behavioural skills as we worked together at various clinics.

Finally, I am grateful to my wife and children for putting up with the writing of this book, and to my secretary, Beverly Beamiss, for deciphering and typing the manuscript.

Preface

This book has been written to introduce professionals working with children to the behavioural treatment of children's problems. It is aimed at practitioners and student practitioners who, not trained or experienced in using behavioural approaches, come across them and wish to find out more about them. It has been written with teachers, social workers, health visitors, child care workers and foster parents in mind.

By using illustrative cases, I have aimed to describe the behavioural approach in action, narrating what a particular course of treatment has felt like in practice rather than giving the kind of clinical and statistical account often found in the journals and textbooks. I have given the initial assessment and treatment formulation work in some detail in many cases; picking the right strategy in the first place is half the battle. Some chapters in the book illustrate standard strategies for a given problem: thus the bedwetting treatment in Chapter 2 is a widely available treatment; the soiling treatment in Chapter 8 (developed by Dr. Gordon Young) is widely applicable to suitable cases; and my own 'paired reading' approach to remedial reading (Chapter 5) is in use in various schools. Other chapters illustrate a highly individualised treatment package for one particular child, as in the self-control treatment described in Chapter 10.

I have drawn upon the case material that I have found useful in illustrating introductory lectures on behavioural treatment, and have tried to present this material here in much the same format as in such lectures. Most chapters give an account of a 'composite' case made up of elements of a number of actual cases to exemplify a particular treatment strategy. All the events recorded have occurred in one case or another. Where a treatment record has been reproduced, it is the record of an actual course of treatment.

I have endeavoured to present each child's treatment together with actual instances of failures, unexpected bonuses, blind alleys and mistakes, as well as planned successes. These all occur in practice, and are better included than left out. They are often highly instructive and it would be unhelpful to give the impression that treatment invariably turns out as initially planned.

One word of warning must be given. This is a book for newcomers to the behavioural field rather than for skilled practitioners. Those readers who wish to start using a behavioural approach with children in their own work are therefore strongly advised to seek the help of an experienced behaviour therapist.

Behavioural treatment is regarded by many as somewhat cold, mechanistic, and simplistic. I, and many other behaviour therapists, once shared that view. Experience of it in practice, however, has shown that it is as warm and human as any other helping approach, that many children positively enjoy it, and that it is an approach many practitioners find works for them. For me, its twin attractions are that it is essentially commonsense rather than mysterious, and that it results in an observable desired effect in a good proportion of cases. There can be little that is more rewarding to a person working with children than congratulating a former bedwetter who has become dry after using an enuresis alarm, or discovering that a child's reading skills have improved and that the child enjoys reading more after a successful period of 'paired reading'.

I hope that this book presents the human as well as the technical face of behavioural treatment.

Cambridge   Roger Morgan
October 1983

One

Introduction to the Behavioural Approach

The purpose of this introductory chapter is to give the reader who is new to behavioural ideas and treatment an overview of the basic concepts and distinguishing features of the approach. It is deliberately brief, since the succeeding chapters illustrate and expand aspects of behavioural work through case descriptions.

Behavioural treatment (or behaviour therapy, behaviour modification, or behavioural casework — terms often used interchangeably but suggesting slightly different contexts or emphases in the use of the same principles) is essentially commonsense and practical. It is devoid of mystique (although unfortunately not always of jargon), and most importantly, it lends itself to being taught to and used by parents and other care-givers rather than to being used solely by psychologists, psychiatrists and psychotherapists.

The first point to underline in describing behavioural treatment is that the term 'behaviour' is used in a technical sense. This use is far wider than the usual 'good' or 'bad' connotation of the word. It is used to describe everything a person says and does, including what he thinks and the emotions he feels; his 'behaviour' is the total of all his actions and reactions, and his 'behaviour pattern' is the collection of his usual actions and reactions. A behaviour problem is any action or reaction which is problematic or unnecessarily distressing — it is not just 'bad conduct'. Inappropriate or excessive anxiety is thus as much a behaviour problem as aggression or stealing.

Behavioural change is the improvement of a problem situation by changing through treatment the ways in which the person usually acts or reacts. Problems may be in areas of development (where a particular behaviour has not developed as it needs to, as with a child lacking reading skills or bladder control), of emotion (involving, for example, inappropriate fears about going to school), or of conduct (where the behaviour pattern is unacceptable to the individual or to others, as in excessive aggression). A judgement is always necessary as to what is acceptable or appropriate, helpful or distressing, and what needs to be changed. The judgement should be shared to the maximum with both child and parents. The practitioner needs, in helping to make such judgements, to have a clear knowledge of what is and is not 'normal' at given ages and in given circumstances, as the yardstick with which any problems can be compared. A basic yardstick for children in normal circumstances can be had from a number of published large-scale surveys of various aspects of behaviour.

There are two key principles in behavioural treatment which together distinguish it from other forms of treatment. The first is that the therapist uses *learning principles* as his therapeutic tool. He aims to improve the situation by *teaching* his patient or client to act or react in different ways, using training tactics and principles which are in most cases derived from the vast amount of experimentation that has been done on the process of learning. This experimentation has led to a body of knowledge known as learning theory, which provides the source for behavioural techniques to be tested in practice.

The second key principle is that of *recording* — monitoring progress (or sometimes lack of it) by keeping objective records throughout of the aspects of behaviour one is trying to change. To do this, one must be very specific in defining the behaviour under consideration, and in defining the goals of one's intervention so that progress towards the known goals can be measured. Recording also requires skill in identifying means of measuring the 'target' behaviour — although it is simplicity, clarity and consistency that are required rather than sophistication. Where the behaviour in question is not amenable to direct measurement, rating scales such as 'is X absent/slight/extreme at the moment' can be used.

Putting these two key characteristics together, behaviour therapy may be defined as the treatment of specific problems, using known principles of learning to teach changed patterns of acting or reacting in problem situations, with objective monitoring of progress towards previously stated treatment goals.

Other psychological treatments concentrate on different features besides the learning process. Thus some therapists would see themselves not as trainers, as behaviour therapists do, but perhaps as detectives aiming to uncover underlying difficulties beyond the observed behaviour — trying to uncover an iceberg beneath the visible tip. Many non-behavioural workers place great emphasis upon *interpretation* of present behaviour or past events. The behaviour therapist, by contrast, does not assume observed or reported problems to be symptoms of any other disorder and he avoids interpretation, confining himself to the task of changing problem behaviours in a measurable way. He does have to make assumptions about what factors might be influencing behaviour, but he tries to make only those assumptions that he can test in practice — such as 'I am assuming X is causing Y to happen, *and therefore* that if I remove X, Y will stop happening'. He will avoid assumptions like 'I believe that by doing A, this child is really expressing subconscious feeling B', because this cannot effectively be either proved or disproved.

An illustration of the difference between a behavioural 'teach changed behaviour' approach and a 'seek the underlying disturbance' approach came from the parent of one of my cases. The child concerned was a boy with some very bizarre behaviours. The parent asked me at our initial interview: 'Can you tell me if he is disturbed. If so, we would of course make allowances and try to help him. If not, then we won't let him get away with behaving like this.' My reaction was that the bizarre behaviour *was* the problem; his 'disturbance' was no more nor less than the bizarre behaviour, and was not some separate underlying entity that we should assume existed as well. Our task was to teach the child how to react to certain situations in a different way (which he wanted to do). In practice, it is quite feasible to remove specified problems by direct training, without the emergence of any other problems to take their place. This suggests that the problem is what is seen, and that it is not some underlying disturbance needing one behavioural problem or another to express itself.

All therapists are interested in the history and development of the problem that they are trying to tackle. The more interpretative therapies place greater emphasis on history as a source of clues to interpretation of the present. The behaviourist is interested in trends in his 'target' behaviours, as background to help in measurement of future progress. He is also interested in past events which might suggest factors which influence the child's behaviour and could be used in a training programme.

Where the origins of a problem can be objectively specified (such as bullying at school leading to fear of school), they are useful to know. This knowledge may, for instance, suggest means of preventing a recurrence of the problem after treatment. However, two facts are relevant here. Firstly, it is rare for the origins of a problem to be objectively known and therefore opinions concerning original causation are usually the result of guesswork. Secondly, one can directly change problem behaviour *without* knowing its cause. Many problems persist long after the original provoking factors have gone, becoming self-maintaining or maintained by external factors, and even certain knowledge of an original cause rarely cures the problem. Knowing that a house caught fire following an electrical fault may suggest prevention of future electrical faults, but still leaves the task of putting out the fire. Similarly, the behaviour therapist is primarily concerned with practical problem alleviation and only secondarily with a search for causes.

One can always speculate on the causes of a problem. It is possible to see many problems in terms of failed or faulty learning in the past — but whether this is the case or not, things can frequently be changed for the better by learning techniques as a treatment.

A typical course of behaviour therapy would follow a sequence such as the following:

1. Specific definition of what the problem is.
2. Decision, involving the child and parents, on the goals for treatment. Should a particular behaviour be changed? How different is it from what is normal for a child of that age and sex, in that situation? In what direction and how far should we aim to change things? (It is worth remembering that the *total* elimination of some problems, such as anxiety, would be quite abnormal.)
3. Design of a recording system to monitor progress, measuring the behaviours of concern.
4. Commencement of this monitoring to measure the severity of the problem before treatment — defining the starting point for later comparison.
5. Analysis of the learning influences currently likely to be affecting the relevant aspects of behaviour.
6. Formulation of a treatment plan comprising appropriate learning procedures and practicable amendments to the existing learning influences, aimed at reaching the agreed goals.
7. Implementation of the treatment plan, and adaptation according to practicalities and records of progress.
8. Phasing treatment out if records show that the goals are being approached.
9. Planning and implementation of any procedures necessary to maintain any treatment effects, or to ensure their transfer to various real life situations outside treatment. This latter is termed generalisation. One usually has to work to maintain and generalise, not just achieve, treatment effects.
10. Replacement of monitoring records by 'follow up' checks to assess maintenance of any progress achieved, and any needs for further treatment.

It is a strength of behavioural treatment that through record-keeping and the definition of goals, success or failure is explicit and measured in all cases. It is worth stressing that one does not have to be a behaviourist to keep records and use them to assess and guide treatment: I believe all types of treatment benefit from objective monitoring, and am saddened that so much treatment — including powerful and often risky drug treatments — is undertaken without the partnership of objective record-keeping of progress and possible problems.

The learning principles used as the behaviour therapists' basic treatment tool are essentially simple and common sense. They are derived from experimental psychology work on learning in animals and human beings, and have been combined and tested in numerous treatment trials. Most treatments involve essentially an extreme focussing of common sense ideas — many of which can be seen in a very unfocussed (and unmonitored) way in everyday child upbringing. Although the basic principles are simple, their effective combination in practice can be highly complex, fraught with risks, and demand considerable skill. Just as in a game of chess a limited number of possible simple moves is combined into a strategy which is adapted to fit a given situation, so in behaviour therapy learning principles are combined into an adaptable strategy according to a behavioural analysis. It is their focussing, consistent application, and adaptation through objective recording that creates their potential effectiveness as a treatment.

Three learning tasks are commonly undertaken in behaviour therapy:

1. the learning of a desired behaviour in which the child is deficient (for example, bladder control, fluent speech, reading skills);
2. the unlearning of an undesired response (for example, facial tics, phobic anxiety, smearing of faeces);
3. the exchange of one response for another (for example, self-assertion in place of tearful withdrawal).

Each of these tasks may be served by one or a combination of four major types of learning:

1. **'Classical' conditioning** or learning by association, in which actions or reactions are changed by repeated new associations: for example, treating bedwetting by using a buzzer device to associate 'holding on' and waking, instead of wetting, with a full bladder; or treating fears and phobias by systematically associating relaxation rather than anxiety with the feared object or situation. (Examples of both types of treatment are given in the following chapters.)

2. **'Operant' conditioning** or learning through consequences, in which the strength and probability of occurrence of an action is altered by changing its consequences: for example, using rewards to build skills in small steps with a handicapped child, or improving reading by systematically praising correctly read words. As may be expected, actions followed by pleasant consequences tend to be repeated more frequently or more strongly. Use of this simple principle, if consistent and systematic, can produce marked changes in behaviour patterns, and the introduction of novel and artificial consequences (for example, small sweets for progress in the performance of a new skill) can, if properly handled, initiate progress which later does not rely upon artificial consequences but secures natural ones (such as social approval) sufficient to sustain it. Any consequence which strengthens a response is termed a 'reinforcer'; consideration of consequences in behavioural analysis often indicates inappropriate reinforcers which may be maintaining a behaviour problem. Reinforcers commonly used in treatment are verbal praise, sweets, various privileges and treats, and 'tokens' which can be 'saved up' for some larger reinforcer. Reinforcers are most effective if given 'little and often', and immediately following the relevant response. In treatment, the required responses are very specifically defined, and complex patterns of behaviour are gradually built up in a large number of small, reinforced steps.

   Possible uses of consequences include: reinforcement of desired responses, non-reinforcement of undesired responses, removal of inappropriately punishing consequences (for example, removal of ridicule following unsuccessful attempts at a task), use of simple punishment (usually a loss of privilege or brief removal from the situation), and reinforcement of an alternative, incompatible behaviour.

3. **'Observational' learning** or learning by example, in which actions or reactions are learned through watching and imitating a 'model': for example, learning social skills by example, or learning to be less aggressive through watching alternative ways of behaving which 'pay off'. Modelling is particularly effective if opportunities are given for reinforced practice of what is learnt. It is particularly useful for the learner to practice the behaviour to be learned alongside his model — known as 'participant modelling'.

4. **'Cognitive' learning** or learning through thinking, in which cause and effect in controlling behaviour are explained, prac-

tised and used to change behaviour: for example, self-control by a child being taught and practicing alternatives to an aggressive outburst, or learning to identify and avoid known problem-provoking situations.

To revert to the analogy of chess, what has been described are the basic 'moves' in behaviour therapy. However, when built into an actual strategy for therapy, things can take an unexpected turn which can catch one unawares. As an example, the idea of reinforcement can be used in helping a young child learn to talk. One simply praises the child when he gets the name of something right. This is clear common sense, and its learning effect as a pleasant consequence is to strengthen the link between object and name in the child's mind. So when my daughter, seated in her high chair, held up the hand she had just removed from a bowl of yogurt and said 'wet', we all applauded. Duly reinforced, she promptly plunged her hands back into the yogurt and looked for further applause. Behaviour occurs in a constant stream and one has to take care about what sequences one is really reinforcing. There is more to chess than just knowing the moves, and the remaining chapters of this book describe some of the things that happen in actual behavioural treatment practice with children.

Two

Paul

Bedwetting — One of the Commonest Problems Of All

Paul was ten years old at the start of his treatment in our weekly bedwetting clinic. The problem of regular bedwetting is shared by one in twenty children of his age — although he did not realise that his problem was so common, because he had never let anyone else at school know about it and the other sufferers amongst his schoolmates had kept their own secret equally well. Paul believed himself to be abnormal, the only boy with his particular problem for many miles around. His parents had heard of other children with the same problem and the family doctor had assured them that it was not at all unusual, but they too considered bedwetting to be far more rare than it is. What was worse, both Paul and his parents feared that bedwetting indicated that he might have serious psychological problems. What little advice they had received had been inconsistent and had failed to relieve Paul of his difficulties.

From Paul's point of view, his bedwetting had become a serious handicap, limiting important aspects of his life. He could keep wetting a secret — but to do so, he had to stay sleeping at home. This meant no cub camps, no school field trips and no staying with friends. He had recently opted out of a coveted place on a school holiday in a youth hostel, hiding behind his father's rescuing white lie that he thought Paul too young to be away from home. His teacher and his friends had accepted this at face value, but to a young boy yearning for his first taste of an adventure away from home, it was the bitter taste of handicap.

When Paul went to bed, his parents allowed him half a cup of cocoa. He was not allowed anything else after tea. He usually slept well in bed, but most mornings the same thing happened. His waking movements sucked cold air into his bed and the resulting chill of soaked pyjamas and sheets confirmed that yet again he had wet his bed. Most days started the same way for him: resigned shame, followed by the trail to the laundry tub with his wet bundle of sheets and pyjamas, and a shower to wash away the wetness in the hope that no-one would catch the smell of stale urine that he knew still clung to his skin. Paul could forget his bedwetting during the busy school day, but occasionally when nothing else was occupying his mind, he worried that his schoolmates or a teacher might notice the smell.

Paul's parents felt that he really should have grown out of bedwetting by the age of ten and that the time had come for him to be properly and fully investigated. Perhaps a bladder abnormality or emotional disturbance needed sorting out. The bedwetting was beginning to exclude Paul from activities that were necessary to his all-round development — hence a visit to the GP and the resultant referral to our clinic.

Before the date of Paul's appointment, a standard letter had been sent out from the clinic asking the family to start a record of wet and dry nights. This was to give us a baseline of his pre-treatment wetting frequency, and a pre-printed chart was provided for the purpose. At the same time we contacted the GP to ask him to arrange two medical checks for us: firstly, to give Paul a physical examination to check for any obvious physical pathology and secondly, to take and have analysed a midstream specimen of urine (MSU) to check for possible infection. We do not treat enuresis without medical clearance on both these counts. Organic pathology is very rare but possible and so should not be missed; however, it is still possible to treat enuresis by standard approaches in many such cases. Some abnormalities popularly blamed for enuresis, such as undescended testicles or circumcision (or lack of it), do not cause wetting. Infections are more frequent but still uncommon and need to be dealt with in their own right. Girls are more prone to infection than boys, because the female anatomy allows easier contamination of the opening of the urethra by faeces — a common source of urinary tract infections. This often shows up on the laboratory culture of the urine specimen as infection by bacteria identified as *E. coli*. Approximately 5% of enuretic girls have a urinary tract infection, and clearing up the infection will cure the wetting as well in about one in three of these cases. However, there is no reason why one should not treat the infection and the enuresis simultaneously.

At his appointment date, Paul's file contained a clear report on his urine specimen and his GP's report of 'NAD' (no abnormality detected) on physical examination.

When Paul was brought into the room by his mother, he was (not unexpectedly) both nervous and somewhat embarrassed at the personal nature of the problem that we were to spend the next three quarters of an hour discussing. I started, as I usually do, by telling him that he was not going to be physically examined again, that we were only going to talk ('like "Mastermind" except you can't say "pass" '), and that he was not alone but one of dozens of bedwetters that I was treating at the time. I told him that at age ten, one out of 20 children wet the bed — so there were likely to be others in his year at school. We proceeded to discuss the physical examination and MSU that his GP had done. As usual, the purpose of these had never been explained to Paul and he did not know their results. Weeing into a bottle appears to be one of those mysterious acts required by clinicians and fulfilled unquestioningly but with embarrassment by small children. Paul was quite interested in my explanation of how the urine was cultured and tested against antibiotics in the laboratory, and he even asked some supplementary questions. He was pleased that his MSU had produced no significant growth when cultured. He was also pleased that he was not going to be examined and I suspect that he spent a few reassuring moments trying to guess who the other bedwetters in his school year might be.

Next, I checked Paul's baseline records. Seven wet nights were recorded out of a total of nine nights — a wetting frequency of 78%. This was the baseline against which to measure any progress (or deterioration) during treatment. Paul also appreciated this on explanation.

We now worked through my standard assessment procedure to clarify the history and nature of Paul's wetting, any other problems of continence, indications of other associated problems, indications of the need for particular adaptations to treatment, and practical issues to be taken into account.

In response to my questions, Paul said that he never wet himself by day. However, he did often need to rush urgently to empty his bladder by day. I asked if anyone ever tickled him, and he agreed that his father often did during rough-and-tumble play together. In response to my direct question, he admitted that on a very few occasions, he had wet the front of his trousers while being tickled. This is 'stress incontinence'. The pelvic floor muscles between the legs are responsible for keeping urine in by keeping the bladder outlet above them pressed shut. When they are unable to do this because the bladder is put under pressure, such as during extreme laughter, the resultant leakage of urine is stress incontinence. With Paul's general urgency to pass urine, this indicated that his pelvic floor muscles were not highly efficient at keeping the bladder outlet closed against a high pressure of urine to escape. This was a likely factor in his wetting, but was not serious; he stayed perfectly dry by day when his pelvic floor was not under pressure and even when being tickled he only leaked slightly, stopping when the laughter stopped and not completely emptying his bladder. All this was explained to Paul — throughout the interview, the relevant body functions and their problems were fully explained to him and all his questions answered. I believe that these explanations to the child are vital to his motivated and intelligent cooperation and persistence in treatment, and that careful explanations at the child patient's level help to ensure full parental understanding of treatment procedures. In enuresis treatment, this is essential for success since parents are the treatment agents and since they are working partly at night when mistakes are all too easily made. Paul, at any rate, became more fascinated than embarrassed and asked increasingly frank and intensely personal questions without self-consciousness. We were beginning to earn his involvement.

Continuing the assessment questioning, Paul's mother confirmed that his bowel control was satisfactory and that he had always wet the bed from birth. About 8 out of 10 bedwetters have never become reliably dry; the others show their poor bladder control by gaining dryness but then losing it again. Both groups respond well to behavioural treatment.

The family had spent much time in the past hunting for regular patterns in Paul's wetting. Frankly, if a pattern has to be hunted for, it is not strong enough to matter. Patterns that need to be taken into account stand out very clearly. In any partially-mastered skill, failures are to be expected on a more or less random pattern, and so will the enuretic wet his bed, without specific causes for specific instances.

Some factors did emerge from questioning as influences on Paul's wetting. He tended to wet more when ill, upset, or under emotional stress — it is very common for any 'shaky' skill to be adversely affected by such factors. Furthermore, he was usually dry when sleeping away from home, for example, at his grandmother's house. Thinking about it, his mother added that precautions taken on past family holidays had usually proved unnecessary, as he had wet less on holiday than at home. I explore this area in assessment interviews because reduced wetting away from home is almost universal amongst bedwetters, and most parents see it as evidence of an element of choice on the child's part — it seems as if he can be dry when he wants to be and is just being lazy at home.

That bedwetting is very commonly less when the child is sleeping away from home — even when in hospital — is nothing to do with choice, but results from the brain's greater alertness to various signals when sleeping in unfamiliar circumstances. Sleep is more easily disturbed by strange sounds when one is away from one's own bed; witness the disturbance most of us experience when sleeping in an unfamiliar place from such things as the creaking of the building, plumbing sounds and traffic noise. Signals about bladder contractions also get through more easily, resulting in better control.

Many believe that wetting is primarily caused by deep sleep. However, sleep has many more complexities and dimensions than simply its depth. Many deep sleepers do not wet the bed and studies have found that enuretic children wet just as often during light sleep as deep sleep. The record of sleep-lightening drugs in treating bedwetting is a poor one. The primary issue is how well the child's brain responds to bladder contractions, rather than how deeply asleep he is.

One possible response to a bladder that is beginning to contract and is ready to empty is to wake up in time, from whatever level of sleep one may be in. Paul said that he did occasionally wake in the night simply to visit the toilet. This was a good sign; one of the normal reactions helping one to stay dry did thus occur naturally at least sometimes and might usefully be strengthened during treatment.

When asked, Paul's mother reported that enuresis ran in her family. Her brother had wet until a teenager, and she remembered frequent 'accidents' at one stage in her own childhood. I explained to Paul that you can inherit a tendency to find bladder control difficult, just as you can inherit tendencies to various other bodily strengths and weaknesses. I made him promise that he would be sympathetic if in the future one of his own children had the same problem.

On the medical side, I ran through a checklist of items that might require a doctor's opinion. Paul's answers suggested nothing untoward that needed referral back to his doctor: he did not 'dribble' urine for long periods after leaving the toilet, experienced no pain or burning or prickling sensations when passing urine (which might have suggested infection), had not noticed blood in his urine, and had no history of urinary tract infections, epilepsy or diabetes. He had not been investigated at hospital for enuresis (some children we saw had undergone X-ray investigations of bladder functioning or bladder-pressure testing, which we needed to ask their own doctors about). Paul had no other physical or psychological difficulties. He was apparently something of a worrier with an occasionally short temper, but nothing outside normal limits.

We then moved to the question of emotional stress. Such stress can disrupt bladder control, or prevent its acquisition, and it was thus important to check that Paul was not suffering stress or facing major changes in his life which might also make treatment less effective.

However, Paul's life, and that of his family, were described as stable and continuing on an even keel.

It is important to underline that the possible effect of stress on bladder control is one of disrupting or inhibiting the process of learning. We all learn and perform learned skills less well if our stress level is too high. This is not the same thing as the widely held idea that enuresis may be a symptom of a deep-seated disturbance. There has been much research on this latter idea and three vital conclusions can be drawn. Firstly, the majority of bedwetters are psychologically completely normal, although more bedwetters than non-bedwetters have emotional problems. Secondly, it is only to be expected that wetting and emotional problems will occur together in some children since both can flow from the same factors — such as family stresses — and, of course, wetting is itself a stress which can lead to other problems. Thirdly, and most important of all, treatments which simply train an enuretic to be dry do not lead to any replacement symptom of disturbance emerging to take the place of enuresis, which is the fear of those who consider that wetting is the outward sign and 'safety valve' of some emotional disorder. It was just such a training programme that I had in mind for Paul.

I now asked about Paul's experience of previous treatments for enuresis. Running a specialist clinic for this problem, I rarely see a 'virgin case' and almost always have to contend with the family's scepticisms born of at least one failed treatment in the past.

Paul had already been given the commonest treatment for enuresis, a prescription for the drug imipramine (Tofranil). This reduces the reactions of parts of the nervous system concerned in bladder contractions. It is also an antidepressant and when used as such carries the side effect of causing urine retention. Paul had also had the commonest response to imipramine. His wetting had reduced dramatically, but had returned again once the tablets ran out. This effect is common to most drug treatments of enuresis: drugs do not produce much lasting change in relevant body functioning. It also transpired that Paul had often forgotten his tablet at night, and that (dangerously) he had on some occasions taken two to make up. Few people take prescribed drugs precisely as instructed — which distorts most doctors' and researchers' assumptions about what dosages did, or did not, produce what results.

I found that his parents had tried the two standard tactics to reduce wetting. They has spent over five years waking Paul every night at their own bedtime in the hope that he would eventually get the idea. They had eventually given this up as useless. It does no harm, but it often is useless; it does not train the child's own functioning and he can come to rely on it. I am amazed that so many parents persist with it for years on end, when the wetting remains obstinately unaffected.

The second tactic was his restricted drinking. Paul was banned any drinks beyond his half cup of cocoa after tea time. There is an obvious but totally incorrect logic to the idea that a boy with less drink going in one end will be less likely to overflow at the other. However, the bladder is not like a tank or elastic balloon that is safer when not too full. It is instead a bag of muscle that actually adjusts to the amount of urine that it is given to hold. The urge to empty is a series of waves of bladder muscle contractions which happen well before the bladder reaches its maximum capacity. The level of urine in the bladder which triggers these contractions — and so the urge to empty — can easily be changed. Reduced drinking tends to adjust the bladder to contract at a reduced level — so reducing the urine it can hold. After an initial adjustment period, increasing Paul's fluids would probably cause his bladder to adjust to holding more. Paul was told to drink as much as he wanted, when he wanted, even at bedtime. Paul clearly approved of this instruction. (However, I am careful nowadays not to say 'drink what you want, when you want', since one patient quoted this in support of a demand to share in the contents of his father's alcoholic drinks cabinet.)

The basic assessment complete, I gave Paul my overall verdict on his problem. I began by asking him if he was good at football. He said he was. The verdict went something like this:

'You are a very normal bedwetter. You are physically normal, and we know you have no signs of infection in your urine. Being a bedwetter does not mean you are odd, babyish or disturbed. You told me you are a good footballer. I'm not — I'm the sort of person who trips over the ball instead of kicking it'. Paul smiled. (It happens to be true, and I'm delighted that I've now found a use for this particular deficiency!)

'Some people are good at football, some are hopeless. Some people are good at bladder control, some are not. I'm bad at football, you're bad at bladder control. It's the way our bodies and brains are made. It doesn't mean either of us is peculiar or disturbed. You were born with a body and brain likely to find staying dry a difficult job — it runs in your family. Keeping urine in is so complicated that it's more amazing that so many people manage it, than that some don't. You don't actually control your bladder as such — that works quite automatically. What you do is to keep the muscles between your legs tight, to keep the outlet of your bladder tight closed and stop urine escaping'. I reminded Paul's mother that she was supposed to have done exercises to retain the ability to control her own bladder outlet at the time Paul was born.

'When you go to the toilet, you open the outlet of your bladder (which points downwards) by pulling down with those pelvic floor muscles between your legs. Then you squeeze your bladder to help it contract and push the urine out, using the tummy muscles all round it and your diaphragm from above. Your diaphragm is the big muscle you use in breathing. Next time you use the toilet, put your hand on your tummy and feel how you start by holding your breath and squeezing with your tummy muscles. Those times you leaked when Dad was tickling you happened because laughing a lot made your diaphragm and tummy muscles press so hard on your full bladder that your pelvic floor couldn't manage to keep the outlet properly closed, and some urine got pushed out. Usually, your muscles cope OK — the only problem you have as well as bedwetting — and it's a slight one — is a bit of daytime urgency. We'll keep an eye on that while we're treating you.'

I explained that what Paul's body and brain needed to do to stay dry at night was to respond quickly and appropriately to bladder contractions, before they built up enough to trigger wetting. Messages about bladder contractions needed to produce two distinct responses from his brain: firstly, holding on by tightening up his pelvic floor to keep his bladder outlet firmly closed against the contractions, and secondly, if the contractions then became stronger instead of dying out, waking him up in time to reach the toilet before his ability to hold on expired.

'This happens properly sometimes, because occasionally you do wake on your own to use the toilet. At other times you can already hold on all right, because you do have some dry nights even without waking. On wet nights, though, your brain is rather like a radio set that is not quite tuned in properly — the messages about bladder contractions don't always get heard. And that's not for lack of trying on your part.'

I told Paul to hold his hands up in the air, then to put them down again. He complied (he was now beginning to enjoy his clinic session). Then I told him to make his heart beat more slowly. Of course he could not. I explained that the difference between lifting one's arms and changing one's heart rate was that the heart is under automatic rather than voluntary control. The point was then made that keeping dry at night is also controlled by automatic mechanisms. A child can no more decide to be dry during sleep than lift himself by his proverbial bootlaces.

Now came the trickiest point in our first session together. I told Paul and his mother that I wished to treat him by using an enuresis alarm. This is often not a popular statement to a family that has heard of failure or already failed with this form of treatment. The enuresis alarm is a much maligned and much misused treatment; while it can achieve success in 80% of cases, it has to be properly used, and is very sensitive to failure if mistakes are made in the necessary procedures.

Paul's mother had suspected my intentions and had clearly heard ill of such devices. She knew that when the child wet a pad placed in his bed, a buzzer would sound to teach him to wake up instead of wetting. This had sounded fine in theory, but she had also heard that in practice the buzzer woke everyone except the child it was supposed to wake, who carried on wetting blissfully unaware of it. Furthermore, she had heard that the buzzer would often sound when the bed was bone dry, and that the metal foil pads in the bed had an unerring tendency to disintegrate into soggy pieces after a week or two of use.

Unfortunately, this is a common tale. Sometimes I surprise parents who have used alarms unsuccessfully before by telling them the story myself. The key point is that such treatment disasters usually arise because of old and poor equipment (I have actually come across equipment using water-soluble materials in the urine detector pads!), little or no instruction to the family in home treatment procedures with the alarm, and no supervision or troubleshooting by anyone experienced in enuresis work.

The pitfalls to be avoided in alarm use can easily be demonstrated. I asked Paul's mother three key questions:

'First, what are Paul's sheets made of?' 'Nylon. It's easier to wash than anything else.' 'Second, does he wear pyjamas?' 'Yes, of course.' 'Finally, if you were downstairs and heard this alarm device go off because Paul had wet, describe exactly what you would do.' 'Wait to see if it woke him, I suppose.' 'If it didn't?' 'Well, that's the problem my friends had with their son. Go upstairs and turn it off myself, I suppose. And wake Paul, because he would be wet, wouldn't he?'

Without further instructions, these three innocuous circumstances could defeat alarm treatment effects. Most children wear nightclothes, and most parents would do what comes naturally in the middle of the night — turn off the alarm noise if after a reasonable time the child hasn't woken. Many bedwetters also have nylon sheets, for the same reason that Paul did. However, nylon sheets are useless with an alarm — they don't let urine through quickly to the detector pad on the bed, and a quick triggering of the alarm as soon as the child starts wetting is essential. They also tend to make children sweat in bed, which triggers false alarms. Because a quick reaction is important, it is also no use waiting to see if the patient is going to wake, then turning the sound off while he is still asleep. If the alarm sound isn't enough on its own, a parent needs to go *quickly* to wake the child before too much time has passed after stimuli from bladder contractions have reached the brain. Waking the child while the sound is still going, then getting him to switch it off, is important to condition the child to respond quickly to the alarm alone. Furthermore, children on alarms should sleep without wearing anything below the waist. Pyjama trousers, long nightdresses, and underpants will all soak up urine before it reaches the detector pad, and so delay the all-important quick response.

Having explained this, I secured agreement to try alarm treatment, on the basis that we would check progress regularly, troubleshoot any practical problems, add or amend procedures if response was inadequate, and persevere so long as continued record charts showed evidence of progress — essentially a very fair treatment contract.

The apparatus was then set up on a clinic couch and demonstrated to Paul and his mother. The urine detector 'sandwich' of two metal gauze mats separated by a sheet was placed under the usual bottom sheet and connected to the alarm box next to the bed. Paul looked disconcerted at the alarm wires, but was reassured that nothing had to be attached to his body.

Paul watched as I held an open bottle of saline over the made up bed. I explained that just before he wet at night, Paul's bladder would start contracting with increasing strength, but without his 'automatic' brain noticing and so without any responses to tighten muscles around his bladder outlet or to wake him up. Then I poured a generous quantity of saline onto the bed.

Nothing happened. Paul watched the spreading wet patch in fascination. His mother concluded to herself that after all the build up, the buzzer was behaving true to the form she had been told about, and had broken down before ever leaving the starting post.

Then the alarm box broke the silence with its customary throaty scream. Paul and his mother jumped. I felt my usual relief on these occasions. Occasionally an alarm does fail to work on such demonstrations, leaving the therapist feeling rather like a bridegroom stranded at the altar waiting for a bride who doesn't show up.

I explained that it takes a few seconds even under ideal circumstances for the urine to soak through sufficiently to trigger the alarm. Pyjama trousers or a nylon sheet over or between the two detector mats delay things very markedly.

After requesting Paul to turn the alarm off, I asked him what he had done the moment that the alarm had gone off. 'I jumped', he said. 'And what happens if something makes you jump in the middle of emptying your bladder?' 'You stop', answered his mother, warming to the subject. 'So, Paul, the alarm makes you jump. Because of the way your body is built, jumping like that makes the muscles between your legs tighten suddenly and cut off the stream of urine. The noise also wakes you up, just as an alarm clock does.'

Mother had begun to look sceptical at this. Both responses do occur automatically to the alarm sound in the majority of children. Where they are lacking, it is possible to add procedures to train the child's body to associate stopping the urine stream or waking, or both with the alarm sound. It is also a common fallacy that enuresis alarms are simply to teach children to wake up. The stream-stopping response is more important in most cases, and many children learn from this response to hold on to the bladder's contents throughout the night without waking. Many bedwetters can be cured without the child ever waking unaided to the alarm.

I continued the explanations at Paul's level. 'The alarm helps you by teaching your brain what to do to keep you dry at night. Can you remember the two things your brain had to do whenever it noticed your bladder beginning to squeeze while you were asleep?'

With a little prompting, Paul recalled that these were to tighten the muscles between his legs to keep the urine in and to wake him up. I explained that these were exactly the two reactions his body would have to the alarm sound — jumping and waking up. After approximately three months of alarm use, his brain should learn to link the 'bladder contracting' message with performing the necessary actions of tightening the pelvic floor muscles and waking up.

The session ended with a recapitulation of procedures to be followed, accompanied by a printed reminder sheet. Paul left holding his alarm and its mats under his arm — somewhat self-conscious and a little afraid people might recognise it. (I keep a supply of plastic dustbin liners in my room for patients too self-conscious to carry out an exposed alarm.) His mother had his wet-and-dry record chart in her bag. From now on this would be the means of monitoring progress against Paul's baseline wetting level of seven wets in nine, and would provide the necessary information for possible decisions about amended or additional treatment procedures to be introduced. It was 25 July.

*　　*　　*

It is worth considering in detail the physiological and therapeutic events that occurred on Paul's first night using the alarm, to appreciate both the therapeutic process and the risks that might, with inadequate prior instruction or subsequent supervision, have made that first night the last:

During that night, Paul stirred and turned as usual in his sleep. His bladder had been filling as bladders do, while he slept, and its muscle walls had automatically relaxed to accommodate the gathering amount of urine without significant increase in pressure. There had been numerous bladder contractions too weak to expel urine through the pelvic floor 'barrier'. However, now the automatic accommodation to increased contents had ceased, the urine pressure was rising as more arrived from his kidneys, and his bladder walls were beginning to contract strongly. If this had happened in the day, he would have been on his way to the toilet by now. At night, however, the signals bombarding his brain had failed to make their point strongly enough. They had disrupted his sleep and made him restless, but they had not succeeded in triggering the safety mechanisms of tightening his pelvic floor or waking him. Paul's bladder contractions reached a peak, his pelvic floor relaxed, and urine began to flow.

As the urine patch spread on the sheet beneath Paul, it also soaked downwards through the sandwich of gauze detector mats, triggering the alarm sound. This registered with Paul, and he did jump, just after his bladder had finished emptying and urine had ceased to flow. He became more restless still, but did not wake. His mother came to him and shook him awake by the shoulder while the alarm sound continued as instructed. She guided his hand in turning it off and then sent him to visit the toilet. He had nothing more to do in the toilet, however. It was all in the bed.

One the face of it, not much had happened. The alarm had worked, but Paul had not woken and had clearly not jumped to the sound in time to stop his bladder emptying completely. The bed was soaked. When it was remade and the alarm switched on ready again, it went off on its own as soon as Paul climbed back into bed. They had forgotten to wipe the plastic sheet dry under the detector sandwich.

The first night was the type that, without detailed explanations of treatment procedures and without regular close specialist supervision, very often culminates in a family giving up and adding another to the list of failed alarm treatments. The usual reason would be 'the thing didn't wake him'. Paul's family, however, had been told that stopping the stream was more important than waking, that most children need parental help in waking, at least at first, and not to expect significant progress within the first month. Besides, they had a second appointment at the clinic in two weeks' time to sort out any problems, and a predicted eight out of ten chance of success: this was the clinic 'track record'. The three-month average duration of alarm treatment was still young. Paul wrote a 'W' on his chart in the morning.

Paul's second clinic appointment came after two weeks on the alarm. The situation looked grim. The record chart showed an unbroken run of wet nights for the entire two weeks. On some nights he had even wet a second time in the same night. On the positive side, however, the alarm routine settled down after the first few nights. Paul was now waking unaided to the alarm. His mother's efforts in waking him quickly while the alarm continued to sound had apparently done the trick and had conditioned him to wake to the noise. He was also clearly jumping and shutting off the urine stream by pelvic floor contraction before emptying completely, because now he had usually a little more urine to produce in the toilet after each alarm triggering.

The run of wets was disappointing, but not that unusual at the start of treatment. The important responses were occurring and building up in strength — he was both inhibiting the urine stream and waking in response to the alarm. We were getting through and now had to wait to see whether, as in most (but of course not all) cases, early basic responses would translate into later dry nights.

One point to arise at this session was that Paul was still very self-conscious about his stale urine smell, particularly now that his enuresis had come more under the spotlight of attention. I suggested using chlorphenesin powder (Mycil) from the chemist, sprinkled like talcum powder over the affected area. It is sold for the treatment of athlete's foot, but also counters the bacteria responsible for the stale urine smell.

After a check that all procedures were being followed as per instructions, we closed the clinic session and Paul and his mother left for another fortnight on the alarm.

Two nights later, Paul had his first dry night on the alarm, followed by a second. Furthermore he slept through the night on both occasions without waking. His bladder probably contracted a great deal at various times as research studies show that the bladders of enuretics do, but the stronger contractions produced the necessary reaction of pelvic floor tightening while the bladder activity subsided. This was all as it should be and suggested that the 'holding on' response was stronger than the possible alternative of substituting waking for wetting. However, none of this was any more than had been happening before treatment, and the two dries were followed by more wets.

A fortnight later, Paul and his mother attended the clinic for the third time. His responses were bearing up well and he was clearly learning from the alarm the prime reaction of holding on as his bladder contracted. Waking was obviously not the key to success in his treatment, although when the alarm went off he woke with little delay and all his mother had to do was help to remake his bed and to make sure that he remembered to visit the toilet. Without guidance, Paul showed an unnerving tendency to try to urinate in the airing cupboard. The wet patches in Paul's bed had now shrunk; no longer reaching from one side of the bed to the other, they were sized something between a 50p piece and the top of a teacup. He had recorded seven wets out of 14 nights since the last appointment — 50% wet and well down on his baseline of 78% before treatment. We were starting to win.

One problem had emerged as the weather became hotter. False alarms had begun to occur, with the alarm sounding on a dry bed. This is caused by the child perspiring, and in hot weather or with continental quilts or overheated rooms, can be the bane of alarm use. Too many false alarms can evaporate cooperation very rapidly. Paul's mother telephoned in for advice and I told her to lessen Paul's bedding, open a window, and above all to change and subsequently wash the sweat-soaked sheets. As an emergency measure, she could double the sheet between the detector mats for greater absorbency.

Because of holiday dates it was three weeks before we next met. It was 12 September. Paul and his family were delighted. There had been no further wets at all. The position can be seen on Paul's own chart, reproduced in Fig. 1. I shared in the delight and declared that Paul was now ready for the final stage of treatment.

This was 'overlearning', which is precisely that. It required Paul to drink as much as he could manage comfortably in the last hour before going to bed, up to a ceiling of two pints. He was to continue using the alarm to 'catch' any further wets and convert them to further doses of learning. Without overlearning, according to our past research, Paul's chances of relapsing to wetting after treatment would be approximately

Morning	Week 1	Week 2	Week 3	Week 4	Week 5	Week 6	Week 7	Week 8	Week 9	Week 10	Week 11	Week 12	Week 13
Wednesday		W	W	D	D	D	D	D	D	D	D	D	
Thursday	W	W	W	D	D	D	D	D	D	D	D	D	
Friday	W_2	W_2	D	W	D	D	D	D	D	D	D	D	
Saturday	W_2	W	D	D	D	D	D	D	D	W	D	D	
Sunday	W	W	W	D	D	D	D	D	D	D	D	D	
Monday	W	W	W	W	D	D	D	D	D	D	D	D	
Tuesday	W	W	W	W	D	D	D	D	D	D	D	D	

Fig. 1 Record of wet and dry nights, kept by Paul (copy of a child's actual treatment records).

one in three. With it, if he could become dry on overlearning, his chances of relapse would fall to approximately one in eight. If he stayed dry on extra fluids, he would be showing a relatively unshakeable level of learned control. If however he wet again, the additional learning effect from further alarm triggerings should build up a safety margin of control. Either way, he should emerge with a more lasting treatment effect. The only risk was that he might be completely thrown by the extra fluids and revert to baseline wetting levels. This is rare, but can happen, so whenever I prescribe overlearning I set an upper limit of three permitted wets in any seven. Any more, and I stop overlearning forthwith and continue on normal intake.

Before ending the session, I again checked procedures — each one, specifically. It transpired that Paul was occasionally wearing pyjama trousers now that he was usually dry. I stressed the need to avoid any lapses in routines that could weaken alarm effects on the rare occasions that it might now go off.

It was again three weeks before the next appointment. Longer than we should have left it on overlearning, but again dictated by late holiday arrangements. Fortunately, the family were able to continue treatment on holiday. (It is amazing how alarms can be used by some families when away. One patient dutifully used his in a tent on a continental camp site. I have always wondered what the other campers thought was going on.)

We met on 3 October. Paul had just one wet night during his three weeks on overlearning. That was a medium-sized patch about the size of a dinner plate, but Paul both woke to the alarm and had more to do in the toilet, demonstrating again the vital pelvic floor contraction. We kept going with overlearning; progress was fully satisfactory and re-newed wetting well within acceptable limits. Futhermore, Paul reported that his daytime urgency had disappeared — probably the result of increased holding ability or to be more technical, a greater functional bladder capacity as he more readily and automatically contracted his pelvic floor against bladder contractions. This time we were able to book in a further appointment for two weeks' time and I gave Paul a target of a final 14 dry nights in a row.

Paul's treatment was proving straightforward. The 'first aid list' of procedures that he might have needed to rescue things and boost progress if his chart had shown no sustained improvement, would have included as a first step a change in alarm sound. This can conveniently, if slightly amusingly, be achieved by putting the alarm box inside an open biscuit tin. If the waking response had been absent or weak, we could have attempted to link the alarm sound and waking by having a parent wake him to the alarm each morning. Poor inhibition of the urine stream (shown by persistently large wet patches and little or no more urine to pass in the toilet afterwards) could have been met by Paul practising stopping in the middle of urination by day to the alarm sound triggered by its test button. A useful range of alternative alarm types now exists, most importantly using different sounds. Different sounds get through to different children. One useful type of miniature alarm can be worn pinned to the pyjama jacket and uses a tiny urine detector plate worn clipped to the front of a pair of underpants for boys, or inside a press-on sanitary pad for girls, instead of the traditional 'in the bed' detector design used by Paul. Such devices are quick-triggering and get through well to the child. The manufacturers of such miniature personal alarms have also produced for me a soundless vibrating alarm to be worn next to the skin, where alarm use needs to be very private, or sound stimuli prove ineffective. Paul's type of alarm has an under-pillow silent vibrator unit and a booster sound, where the standard stimulus doesn't work.

However, these tactics and devices could remain on the clinic shelf as far as Paul's treatment was concerned. When he returned to see me on 17 October, he had achieved over 14 consecutive dry nights on over-learning.

'Congratulations, Paul. I officially declare you a dry boy.' I shook a happily grinning Paul by the hand, and told him that he could now give the alarm back, and from now on could revert to normal (but not restricted) drinking.

A happy, dry boy left the clinic after 12 weeks of successful effort — with a 7 to 1 chance he would not need to return. The alarm box went back into the clinic cupboard, soon to be reissued to the next enuretic patient. Paul took his used gauze mats home with him, destined soon to form a temporary front to his mouse cage.

Three

Gary

A Fear of School

I was asked to help Gary, his family and his school to overcome his severe fear of going to school, which had led to his total absence from school for the previous two months.

I first met Gary on a visit to his home, where I talked over the problem with him and his mother. Father was present, but left most of the talking to mother. Gary was a rather small and reserved eight year old, but clearly interested in what I had to say, wanting to stop being frightened of school, and willing to answer my questions. In the last chapter, Paul was a relatively 'routine' behavioural case, with a common problem. A standard treatment strategy was available to him, backed by guidelines from research work with large groups of children and simply needing to be tailored to suit the particular boy in question. It is relatively easy to become a skilled therapist at a given treatment 'package' like the enuresis alarm. However, Gary presented a different and more challenging problem altogether. He was a 'one-off' case for which one had to do a full analysis of relevant behaviour patterns, and to create — and keep modifying — a unique treatment package out of the available learning tactics. My aim in this chapter is to show how one can go about this — warts and all.

The first task, after gathering details of the family makeup, was to define Gary's problem as precisely as possible. 'He doesn't go to school' is far too vague, even if correct. It leaves too many unanswered questions and too many possible variations in the problem. We needed to define the *frequency* of the problem, its *intensity*, its precise *nature* ('what would a video camera record him doing' helps to focus an account of what actually happens), and the *duration* of any relevant incidents. The mnemonic 'FIND' helps to guide this part of the assessment.

Gary's frequency of school non-attendance was easy to check from the school register. Before the last half-term, he had attended 62 half-days out of a possible 74. The first week after half term, he had attended five half-days out of the possible ten, the next week he had attended six, the third week two, and with one half-day's exception, he had not attended school at all for the subsequent seven weeks to date.

This information gave us our 'baseline' record of how bad things were before treatment, against which we could measure any subsequent progress. It is often difficult to secure a reliable and reasonably lengthy baseline record (one has to postpone treatment to do it, which is often neither easy nor acceptable). Here, however, Gary had a problem that had already been recorded permanently for us.

The intensity and nature of the problem were discussed together in our interview. During the early days of the problem, Gary's mother had tried to take him to school. A video camera would have recorded Gary pulling away from his mother as they entered the school gate, being pulled up the path by his mother who would be partly telling him off, partly reassuring him, and partly pleading with him. Eventually Gary would pull himself free of her once at or inside the building. He would then run out of the school gate, screaming until back on the pavement outside. His mother would follow and take him back home. After a run of days like this (I could not determine the precise number), his mother had — perhaps forgivably — given up the obviously unsuccessful attempts and a video camera at school would never have spotted Gary at all from then on. He would simply be at home, playing, reading comics, watching television or, as his mother put it, 'generally getting under my feet or up to mischief'. The next day I checked with the school on this account of the nature and intensity of Gary's 'not going to school' (which was now clearly resolving into apparent fear and running from school as well as straightforward 'non-attendance' — obviously a quite different picture from behaviour such as truancy). The headteacher confirmed Gary's mother's account. He said that each time Gary's mother had tried to bring him to school, Gary had run from the building screaming, even before he reached the cloakroom to remove his coat.

To complete the picture of the problem, I asked mother to describe what happened at the home end of an attempt to take him to school, as well as the school end. Apparently he displayed sullen refusal to get ready for school or leave the house, withdrew from the remainder of the family, pleaded tearfully to be allowed to stay at home, and inevitably discovered that he had 'lost' essential items of school clothing like his outdoor shoes, or the gym kit that simply *had* to be taken that day. He also frequently complained of stomach pains or nausea.

On duration of relevant incidents, it was relevant to note that Gary's screaming usually ceased once he was on the way home out of the school grounds, and that stomach aches, nausea and tears ceased once he was allowed to remain at home. This is *not* to say that Gary was 'putting it all on', he clearly had an abnormal reaction to school, and he did not enjoy his fear of school. Many of us experience stomach upsets when faced with anxiety-provoking situations, which right themselves as soon as the 'danger' is past. This makes them no less genuine. However one might be tempted to interpret Gary's observable behavior, and as a behavior therapist one would avoid the gratuitous guesswork of personal interpretations; it was a behaviour pattern Gary said he wanted to change — and subsequently worked upon very hard.

The school records gave us the recorded history of Gary's attendances. However, we did probe further in discussion into the history of the problem, in case a possible trigger event could be identified. This might have indicated a situation to be avoided in the future. Furthermore, a trigger event might have suggested a particular angle by which to approach treatment or a current situation to be relieved if we were to make progress. For Gary, this line of investigation yielded nothing. This is usually the case in my behavioural practice — despite the common assurances in so many accounts to the effect that 'it all started when X occurred'. Even when some possible trigger does emerge in discussion, often I find that it bears little logical relationship with the problem it is supposed to have precipitated, and that proclaiming them cause and effect seems something of a leap in the dark. Gary had simply developed an aversion to school, starting suddenly and developing rapidly, with no triggering events that anyone could identify.

The next vital step was to identify desirable treatment goals for Gary. There was little difficulty over this — we all agreed that our goal was to restore Gary to regular school attendance *without* experiencing fear. Most important, Gary himself accepted this goal. Once one of my students remonstrated with me over this type of goal, taking the radical view that children like Gary were demonstrating a justifiable rejection of educational values and processes unsuited to their needs. I am afraid that I have little time for that kind of view; in the real world, the consequences for Gary of continued fear of school and school non-attendance were possible removal from home, not a revolutionary change in the British educational system. He and his family asked me to try to take away a fear that impacted upon his participation in the normal daily life of a schoolboy. That is a perfectly acceptable request for treatment.

One final precaution, before starting on the analysis of Gary's problematic behaviour pattern, was to check whether he had any other problems that we should take into account. This is particularly important with the more physical problems like speech disorders, wetting or soiling — in such cases it would be necessary to know whether there were any related physical or developmental problems. With non-attendance at school, the areas of possible relevance are less clearcut, but needed investigation all the same. Possible lines of relevant investigation included a check for reading difficulties or for difficulties in social relationships with other children.

A discussion with school staff revealed that Gary was a 'remedial reader' — though he had lost his place in the remedial group through non-attendance. One way of eliciting definite judgements from one's informants is to ask them to complete rating scales. I asked Gary's teacher to rate him on a number of factors — such as ability to mix well with others (where she had to choose between five possible answers ranging from 'very poor', through 'average', to 'very good'). She rated him 'well below average' in overall school attainment, 'average' in ability to mix, and 'worse than average' for classroom behaviour. Our discussions did not reveal any major problems at school that might be blamed for putting him off going there. He was not known to be the victim of bullying and he had come reasonably to terms with his new teacher over the previous half-term. In addition to these probing discussion sessions at home and school, and the completion of my home-made rating scales, I asked Gary's mother and teacher to complete a standard published behaviour rating scale. This indicated that Gary had a range of behavioural problems, many of them of a mildly or moderately antisocial nature.

Gary was no angel and, despite being small and reserved, clearly had a number of fairly unattractive attributes. Apparently he was not averse to bullying others on occasion. Discussion of the completed behavior scales and the various reported problems at home and school however confirmed non-attendance, and incorporating observed fearful avoidance of school, as our target problem. It was the most serious problem of a boy with a range of problems.

We now progressed to a behavioural analysis centering on this target problem. Throughout this, it must be borne in mind that although we were now focussing on Gary's main problem, at all times we acknowledged that Gary had other problems and indeed as a whole the family had other problems — in relationships, housing and finances. As a behaviour therapist, one selects a defined issue to work on; if one is successful with a child who has multiple problems, at least one has removed one problem and can start on another.

The term 'behavioural analysis' is an impressive piece of jargon. Essentially it means getting enough information about the problem actions or reactions and about the other actions and circumstances surrounding them, to be able to formulate some specific ideas about what may be influencing what. This formulation serves the sole purpose of suggesting changes that one might make in the various actions and circumstances surrounding the problem behaviour in order to improve it in the direction of the agreed goal. At this point one must make a testable prediction along the following lines: 'my formulation of what factors might be influencing the problem behaviour suggests that if I change factor X in manner Y, then the problem behaviour will change in desirable manner Z'. The object of the whole exercise is to secure Z, thus Z must be measurable so that one can tell if one is succeeding or failing. One has also now moved neatly from assessment of the problem and its influencing factors on to a treatment plan — namely 'change X in manner Y'. The value of the testable prediction that 'Z will then occur' is that if Z is achieved all is well. However, if Z is not achieved, then one has an immediate indication that the treatment needs to be changed. If Z is achieved, it does not actually matter at the time whether the initial behavioural analysis was over-simplified or wrong — one would simply have hit on the right treatment for the wrong reasons. The original analysis, however, is the source of ideas on how to achieve Z. If it does not suggest anything practicable and effective, it has failed and one starts again to reanalyse — usually trying to secure more accurate information about various aspects of behaviour (perhaps by doing more direct observation of what the child is doing and relying less on the reports of others). When they are done properly, I have found behavioural analyses carried out to the plan described below very serviceable in producing effective ideas for treatment.

To analyse Gary's school non-attendance, I began with a clean sheet of paper and the file of information about his actions and their surrounding events, described as objectively as possible. Then I used the ABC model of analysing a behaviour pattern. A stands for antecedent events — those that lead up to the problem behaviour, B for the set of problem behaviours, and C for consequent actions and events. This is my own approach and many adopt it; there are different approaches which other therapists find suit them.

The first step was to define B, Gary's problem behaviour. This could be defined as: (1) signs and statements of anxiety, (2) running back out of school, usually screaming, and (3) actions likely to prevent a journey to school (for example, 'losing' school clothing). These were written under B in the centre of the page.

A circle had to be drawn around these B definitions. Behaviour occurs within a person, and the analysis sheet is needed to record any particularly relevant characteristics of that person. The key characteristics labelling Gary's circle were poor academic skills and a wider range of behaviour problems. (It did not apply in Gary's case, but any physical characteristic leading to being teased at school could have been highly relevant here.)

On the left, the A (antecedent) events were then filled in. These were the preparations to go to school and approaching and being taken into the building. I made a mental note that these may need breaking down further later on, and that additional details might suggest possible changes that might affect the B reactions. Might it make a difference, for instance, if Gary were taken into the building by his brother or if he went to school through a different entrance? Such simple variations should not be discounted as possible treatment tactics.

The consequent events, C, of Gary's problematic reactions to going to school were written on the right. Here, it can prove very fruitful to identify possible pay offs (not necessarily realised by those involved) earned by the problem behaviour. After Gary had either avoided the trip to school altogether or run back home, the C events included the disappearance of signs and statements of fear. (This one is easy to miss, but it is potentially important and worth looking for wherever the target problem involves anxiety. Escaping from an anxiety-provoking situation can be a strong pay off.) There was also a range of probably pleasant activities such as watching television. Later I observed for myself that his mother gave him a packet of crisps each time he had run from school — to 'make up for having dragged him off there when he was afraid'. This was enough for the first formulation; if necessary we could go into more detail and produce with Gary's help a balance sheet of the good and bad consequences of staying at home versus going to school. It is always worth having such contingency plans for further analysis up one's sleeve, although in Gary's case a useful treatment plan emerged without needing to go into this further detail.

The analysis summary sheet now appeared as shown in Fig. 2. The ABC sequence across the page showed the flow of behaviour as we had

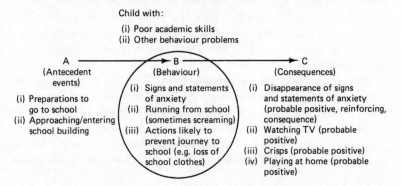

Fig. 2 ABC behavioural analysis of Gary's non-attendance at school.

defined it so far. We now turned our attention to two final elements of the ABC model of behavioural analysis. Firstly, to possible factors (perhaps the presence or absence of certain people) which might increase or reduce the likelihood of Gary's school avoidance. Such factors are labelled in the jargon as 'discriminative stimuli'. In practice, they serve rather like traffic signals, encouraging or inhibiting the ABC behaviour sequence under analysis. A simplistic but helpful example is that the likelihood of a boy stealing apples from an orchard is very much affected by who else may be present. The presence of a playmate may encourage the stealing sequence. The presence of a policeman will clearly discourage the same sequence. The playmate and policeman are the two types of discriminative stimulus — the 'go' and 'stop' signals respectively for a given behaviour sequence. An example in the therapeutic world is the presence of the husband or wife of a person suffering anxiety in social situations; the husband or wife is often a discriminative stimulus making the anxiety sequence and its associated behaviour less likely to occur. For Gary, we recognised that the presence or absence of particular family members, mother or brother perhaps, may serve as effective traffic lights for the sequence. This was to prove vital at a later stage of my work with Gary. One twist to bear in mind was that my own presence could well become a discriminative stimulus affecting Gary's school behaviour. Potentially this could become either a useful tool or a real hindrance.

The second element was the background situation in which all the other ABC events occurred. Most behaviour patterns, normal or otherwise, are specific to certain situations. For example, our own conversational behaviour and the words we use vary greatly from one social situation to another — we tend to have one pattern at home, another at work, and perhaps another at the pub or club. Usually children display very different patterns at home and at school, and there is often little overlap between behaviour problems shown in one situation and the behaviour shown in another. This last point gives rise to the rather foxing statement made so often to a therapist checking a child's behaviour in a new setting; 'I can't see what the problem is supposed to be — he doesn't do that with me!'

This situation effect on behaviour has both advantages and disadvantages when one is treating a problem. On the positive side, it is always worth considering a change in situation as a possible therapeutic ploy — to see if the same drama occurs on a new stage. For Gary, this would mean trying him in a new school setting — a new school or at least a new class. On the negative side, as a therapist one often finds that one has succeeded in producing a desirable change in a given setting, only to find that it won't generalise to any other setting. One has to plan and work not only for the desired change, but also to make it transplantable. This was later to put a spoke in my otherwise successful efforts to help Gary.

Once the analysis was complete and plotted on paper, the next step was to produce the formulation of what factors might be influencing Gary's problem, according to standard research-derived learning principles. My initial formulation was that Gary was responding with anxiety to the school situation (and possibly also to separation from his mother), and that avoidance of school attendance was probably being reinforced and so maintained by payoffs including anxiety reduction (on 'escaping' from the prospect of a day at school) together with attractive alternatives such as television and the opportunity to play at home.

Building on this formulation, somehow my treatment plan had to graft a desired new B behaviour of anxiety-free school attendance onto Gary's behaviour pattern in the place of the existing B behaviours of school avoidance and anxiety. To make this graft stick, I needed to create new elements in the ABC sequence strong enough to supplant the existing A–B and B–C links identified in Fig. 2.

I had to link school attendance to the same antecedent events that I had already identified — namely preparing for school and approaching and entering the building. And I had to make this new behaviour stronger than the existing problem one. I decided to attack this problem at both ends. At the A–B end of the sequence, I planned to weaken the A–B link between the antecedent events and anxiety/school avoidance by reintroducing Gary to school in extremely small, but progressive, steps — each one chipping away at the unwanted A–B link. There is good evidence that taking a feared task in steps small enough for each one to be coped with gradually does whittle away anxiety. One becomes less and less sensitive to the anxiety producing stimulus or situation as one becomes steadily accustomed to it. The process is known as 'desensitisation', and forms a common behavioural gambit. Chapter 6 describes a case entirely based on this approach. To strengthen the new A–B link to school attendance, I planned also to encourage in Gary some reactions to school which would be incompatible with anxiety. There were a number of possibilities to choose from, since there is an almost standard range of 'anxiety inhibiting responses'. These include deliberate muscular relaxation, vigorous physical activity, and eating food. However, for Gary I decided on the tactic of engaging him in 'fun' activities as part of the approach to school. These could include travelling in my car (fun since he loved cars and the family did not have one) and pretending to be television hero characters marching off to battle as we walked up the road to school. If I could make him laugh as he went to school, I would be counteracting his anxiety.

At the B–C end of the sequence, I needed to arrange some powerful pay offs at the end of the new ABC chain that I wanted to create. To do this, I opted to use cardboard tokens which Gary could earn each time that he achieved one of his steps towards school attendance, and which I would redeem later for real money to buy items he wanted at the local corner shop. Tokens are useful reinforcers for desirable actions because they are so flexible. They can be given at the appropriate time, and like real money, are valuable because they are 'backed up' with the power to purchase items (or perhaps some other form of treat).

At this point, some readers may baulk at the idea of rewarding behaviour change. To some it smacks of bribery. However, those who reject the idea of rewarding progress in adapting behaviour usually accept the concept of punishing 'bad' behaviour. Where one is trying to develop a child's skill (for example, in reading or becoming clean or dry), or to dismantle a problem such as inappropriate anxiety, I see nothing wrong in using the established fact that pleasant outcomes reinforce success, strengthen it, increase it, and maintain it. In other circumstances where one is aiming to encourage a child to 'be good', I believe it more, and not less, acceptable to do this by agreeing to make 'being good' have pleasant consequences, rather than by arranging punishments for *not* being good — particularly as the former tactic is usually more effective in producing change. One must also emphasise that the reward has to be earned — progress has to be made in order to secure it.

Figure 3 shows these treatment plans in ABC form — Gary's initial problem and treatment diagram. Actual progress (achievement of school attendance tasks, together with levels of observed and reported anxiety) would dictate when and whether I needed to rethink this picture. I made the treatment prediction, to Gary and his parents and to the school, that he would attend school for progressively increasing periods up to the normal school day, eventually without reporting any anxiety. Having declared one's goals and set up a recording system to show whether progress towards them is being made, the behaviour therapist really does make his success or failure rather blatantly public!

As a final therapeutic tactic, I wished to change Gary's school class. He was pleased at this prospect, and the change of setting brought us the possibility of a different behaviour pattern. It was just possible that

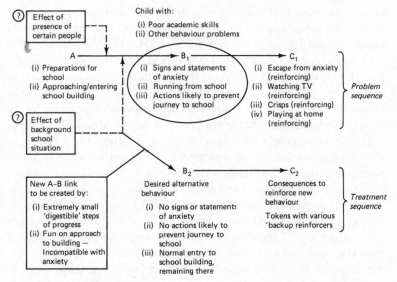

Fig. 3 Treatment plan for Gary.

Gary might attend school if he was to join a new class, and he did admit to some disagreements between his past teacher and himself.

*   *   *

Having completed this theoretical basis, it was time for the treatment to 'go live' with Gary. I visited the school and a willing but sceptical headteacher agreed to my various ploys, including the change of class. Effectively I was given the run of the school with Gary, and it was agreed that when Gary completed one of my 'steps to school' tasks, he would be officially registered as having attended school. (This was important, since proceedings for non-attendance were becoming likely.)

Gary himself agreed to my treatment plans — only on condition that I would not make him go into class yet and only after a great deal of reassurance. He and I negotiated our first day's treatment agreement together: I would collect him from home in my car, we would run together through the school grounds, in one gate and out of the other, and then drive home. If we succeeded, I would give Gary a token to put in the tin that he had found for the purpose. He decided that he would save his tokens towards a jacket for his Action Man toy soldier, which we agreed would be worth ten tokens.

On day one, I arrived at the house to find Gary unwilling to come to school without his mother and brother. So we all got into the car and visited the school. It was the middle of the afternoon. We stopped outside the school gate and, leaving the rest of the family in the parked car, Gary and I went in through the first gate. The 'fun element' this time was a race — I challenged Gary to beat me in running to the other gate. He clearly enjoyed the game (he won the race!) and proceeded to exceed expectation by re-entering the grounds to show me the door that he usually entered by. We returned to the car, where I gave him plenty of congratulations, and his first token towards the Action Man jacket.

Day one had gone well. Apprehensive at the start, Gary had more than completed his agreed task and had enjoyed it rather than experiencing anxiety. The latter was vital; clearly we had kept the countermeasures to anxiety (the car ride, the fun of the race, and the reassuring presence of family and perhaps by now of myself) strong enough to win any battles with anxiety. The net result was enjoyment rather than fear. Theoretically, if I could keep things enjoyable as I gave Gary gradually increasing 'doses' of school each day, an association of enjoyment with school should gradually build up, and the association of fear with school should become weakened. In terms of learning theory jargon, I should be 'conditioning' Gary to respond positively to school, displacing and thus 'counter-conditioning' his anxiety, avoidance and escape responses. The praise and tokens should help this process along by reinforcing the new ABC route along which I was trying to divert Gary's behavioural flow. If only I could keep using fun as a barrier to anxiety and tokens and praise as magnets to attract school attendance.

These were the thoughts running through my mind on the drive home after dropping Gary and his family back at their house. The theory was fine, but in practice there were still many ifs and buts to it. My ideas about making it fun for Gary could fail, the tokens could prove too weak a reinforcer to override the pay offs already there for running away from school, and I could all too easily blow everything by one day giving Gary too big a dose of contact with school, provoking a destructive dose of anxiety which might trigger him to run away from me too. These dangers could create all the wrong associations in a very short space of time and effectively throw the treatment effect into reverse. It was also possible that Gary might, as some children do, react quite unpredictably. He might demonstrate the initial formulation to be useless, or on the positive side, might start attending school again in his new class as suddenly as he had stopped attending last half-term. His mother's influence on the problem remained something of an enigma: she was strongly associated with Gary's school fears, and might even be a 'green traffic light' discriminative stimulus for them;

she reinforced his escape from school, yet (as would be expected) her presence helped to inhibit anxiety too. In discussion, she was very fed up with the way Gary had embarrassed her in front of the other mothers at school and she wanted to leave the job of getting him back there up to me. I decided to accept that, at least at this stage, and to work out an effective strategy in practice that I could eventually hand over to her.

On a lighter note, the case had one factor in it of the sort one doesn't usually read about in the literature. I was myself apprehensive in Gary's house, because the family owned a huge monster of a guard dog called Rex. Rex's chief occupation appeared to be snarling at behaviour therapists. Now I like dogs — little pet ones like Scottish terriers and corgis or big friendly ones like retrievers — but Rex was not that sort of animal. Gangster films have characters known as hired guns. Rex was hired teeth. One day I took a student psychologist with me to Gary's home. When Rex bounded out *over* the garden gate and stood snarling through the windscreen with his forepaws on the car bonnet, my student flatly refused to leave the car or to accompany me on this particular case again. My peace of mind was hardly eased when my Sunday newspaper announced that guard dog breeders were starting to cross-breed alsatians with wolves.

The agreed task for day two was for Gary to walk with me through the school building — without stopping — during school hours. As happened throughout treatment, he and I had negotiated and agreed the size of the next step at the end of the previous session. I was aiming each time to achieve a modicum of progress, either through a slightly bigger 'dose' of school, or by a slight reduction in the anti-anxiety support that I was providing. On day two, Gary's mother (by prior agreement) did not come with us, but his older brother did. Although I found Gary in tears at the prospect when I arrived, he came, the tears stopped once we set off, and the task was completed to earn a second token.

On day three, Gary, his brother and I met the headteacher by arrangement and looked with him through the glass door panel into the class Gary was to join. This presented no difficulties and I gave Gary his congratulations and token as usual. On the way home, Gary declared that he could never face entering that classroom when it was full of other children. However, he did accept the task for day four of exploring the room with me after school, when everyone else had gone home.

At the start of day four (late in the afternoon), Gary said he felt very afraid and hid in the toilet at home before agreeing to come to the school provided that his mother came too. She agreed, so we all set off for school. Gary was reluctant to leave his mother in the car, but soon agreed to join me in the empty school. We explored the classroom for some time, Gary becoming fascinated with some of its equipment. Best of all, for both Gary and me, was the class hamster. Gary was delighted with it and wanted to visit the hamster again the next day. Good: school was beginning to become associated with some positives for Gary — and I regarded the innocent animal as a welcome extra reinforcer for Gary's entry into school!

The next day's assignment would be a key barrier to be overcome. I had to bring Gary into school in the presence of other children — a make or break stage for our treatment. Gary agreed to visit the school at the end of the school day and to come with me *briefly* into the classroom of children. However, he did make three conditions, all of which I accepted as valid anxiety-inhibitors: I was not to leave him alone, his mother could wait in the car outside, and he could feed the hamster. This latter was unplanned, but a godsend as both an anxiety-inhibitor and a reinforcer.

As I drove to the house on the Friday afternoon, day five, I resolved to increase the anxiety-inhibitors and the fun element of going to school as much as I could. I would let Gary play the car radio at full pop music volume (a request I had declined in the past!) and on the way to the building I would introduce the idea of pretending to be two television characters marching into battle, in the hope that I could engage Gary in fun play-acting and divert him from mounting anxiety as he approached his Rubicon.

Things were not auspicious at the house. Gary reported tearfully that he was afraid, that he had both a tummy ache and a headache, and that one of his outdoor shoes had gone missing. I tried to reassure him, telling him that the task was always all right when he tried it, reminding him of the tokens for the Action Man jacket, and generally trying to be friendly, sympathetic and supportive to a crying, frightened little boy. 'He won't go while the other kids are there, you know' said his mother, not entirely helpfully. Inwardly I convinced myself that I had pushed Gary too far too fast. He was upset and not to be moved.

On the point of giving up, I realised that I was making a cardinal mistake and not helping Gary at all by my reassurances. When stuck on a case 'in the field', the main source of ideas on what to try next is one's original behavioural analysis. In this case, I had identified reinforcers maintaining the problematic and upsetting ABC sequence of anxiety/non-attendance, and the whole drive of my treatment efforts was to build up, reinforce and maintain a new ABC sequence of anxiety-free school attendance. Yet here I was doing precisely the opposite. I was pouring in sympathy and support for anxiety and refusal to leave the house, instead of supporting departure for school. I was reinforcing Gary's anxiety and school avoidance.

To reverse this mistake, I left Gary and announced that I would ignore him until he started getting ready for school, and that I would leave, with or without him, in five minutes. I also listed the reinforcers for going to school: radio, car ride, hamster, token — and now play-acting.

I ignored Gary and ensured that his mother did as well by the simple expedient of asking her to tell me about her latest argument with the housing department. As soon as Gary left the settee, I praised him effusively. He stopped sobbing and 'found' his lost shoe. I praised him while he put it on. I must admit that he took a full five minutes to get ready and that I 'extended' some of the minutes to rather more than 60 seconds. I must also admit that at the time I was not very sure that I would eventually be recording the occasion as a successful correction to a treatment programme in a chapter such as this. However, come Gary did: he stopped crying, stopped complaining of headache or stomach ache, and within minutes was sitting in the car on the way to school, gleefully turning the radio volume to maximum on the pop music station.

At this point, it is worth pausing to consider the emotional side of what had happened. Technically, I had switched my (probably) reinforcing attention from the undesirable ABC track to the desirable one (see Fig. 3). This makes logical sense. Emotionally, however, I had been reacting in a fatherly fashion towards a distressed eight year old and then had to stop being sympathetic. That was hard to do. The emotional results, however, are vital. Gary stopped crying within a couple of minutes of my ignoring him; yet he had cried much longer than this during my efforts to reassure him. As a therapist, I was there for the sole purpose of reducing anxiety and enabling him to come to school and the differential reinforcement approach that I had switched to appeared to have achieved this. I was not there simply to be fatherly. Sometimes therapeutic strategies have to be more logical than instinctive. However, the fact remains that *less* sympathy directed to Gary's school anxieties and more attention to school's positives — like feeding hamsters — had shortened rather than worsened Gary's distress that Friday afternoon.

As we walked from the car into the school after our brief but noisy journey, I brought the diversionary fun activity of pretending to be fictional characters into play. Gary and I pretended to be Action Men storming enemy territory, with shouted commands and battle cries between us.

Fortunately (for me!) few people witnessed our unconventional approach to the school and, more fortunately, Gary fully entered into the spirit of the play-acting. Going into school was a game, for a boy who twenty minutes earlier had been sobbing on the settee about it. We were making progress.

As Action Men, we 'stormed' the classroom door and entered the classroom — somewhat to the surprise of the children. (I managed to switch Gary's interest from Action Man to the hamster at this point!) By play-acting at an eight year old's level, I had managed to hold anxiety at bay sufficiently to get Gary into a classroom full of children. Of course, the occasion and our behaviour was artificial — but in treatment one can often introduce enough artificial props to achieve what is wanted, and then phase out the props afterwards as the achievement becomes more established.

Many of the children in the class asked if Gary could have his place next to them. This was reinforcing for Gary. One boy called an insulting nickname and I countered this by whispering to Gary that I wanted him to ignore it. I told him that the boy would try a few more times, then give up if he got no reaction. This happened as predicted. Gary was allocated a desk next to a boy called Damon, and then we left. On leaving the class, Gary promised to see Damon 'for a few minutes' the next school day.

We returned home in the car and Gary had his fifth token. Week one had seen Gary enter a classroom full of children, willingly, without reported or observed anxiety, and looking forward to his next visit. We had crossed a Rubicon.

In week two, I began taking Gary to school for increasing periods in class, always taking him during the afternoon and taking him home at the end of the normal school day so that premature departure or 'escape' from school was never reinforced. I continued the approach of paying him attention only when he was actually getting ready for school, and strengthened the reinforcement for getting ready by providing sweets or peanuts whenever he was in the car ready to leave in less than his alloted five minutes from my arrival at the house. I had to do this partly because I was now finding it impossible to prevent his mother from remonstrating with Gary when he was refusing to get ready. To some extent the sweets or peanuts were a counter to this, strengthening the pay offs for going to school in the face of the possibly reinforcing attention to school avoidance. During week two, I also began phasing out Gary's artificial props by leaving him in the classroom while I went outside for short but increasing periods.

Monday of week two was successfully achieved: Gary spent 25 minutes in class and I left him without my support (by prior agreement with him) for five minutes. On Tuesday Gary spent 55 minutes in class and I left him alone there for the final 20 minutes, meeting him at the door with the parents of other children at the end of the day to take him home. On Wednesday he spent one and a half hours and a playtime at school, now giving me an agreed 'secret signal' when he was happy for me to leave. As usual, I collected him after school. Thursday saw a full afternoon's attendance at school, without reporting any anxiety and without me being present at all. I simply dropped him off after lunch and collected him after school.

During the first part of our second week, two concessions were agreed with the school to avoid identified 'anxiety points'. Firstly, it was agreed that Gary could remain in the classroom at playtime (later he naturally drifted into the playground with the other children, but at first he was nervous about playtimes). Secondly, he was given leave for a time to watch rather than join in activities in the gymnasium, which also worried him particularly. A new positive also developed over the week, helping to reinforce and make pleasant Gary's time at school. He became firm friends with his classmate Damon who, quite unprompted, encouraged and praised Gary over difficult patches and who served as a very useful model of how to cope with the ups and downs of the school day. Provision of models from whom to learn coping skills is often contrived as part of a treatment programme; here it was tailor-made already in Damon. As necessary I specifically encouraged Gary to observe how Damon coped with particular issues.

But however careful a treatment planner one may be, treatment can be made or broken by the unexpected. Fate was not to let me become complacent. Day ten was a disaster. The task was for Gary to have school lunch (with me present) and then to stay alone for the after-noon's lessons. Gary was extremely anxious about eating lunch at school, and although each day so far his initial anxiety before leaving home had ceased within the allotted five minutes, today it did not. I could not get him to leave the house at all and we had to abandon the day's task.

After a weekend to consider the equivocal progress of week two, I opened week three with the task of an afternoon alone at school, arriving after lunch. This was something Gary had already achieved, and he achieved it again with no problem at all. It was also helpful that Damon's presence as a supporter and friend was making my own presence unnecessary to reassure Gary and inhibit anxiety in the classroom itself. This was proving an incalculable bonus which must have contributed largely to success. Gary now had his tenth token, so we stopped to buy the Action Man jacket on the way home, and decided on the next 'back up reinforcer' to be earned by the next set of tokens for completed tasks.

It was time for consolidation rather than pushing ahead too fast, so I repeated the 'afternoon only' task twice more — without difficulty — before trying a school lunch again. This time we achieved it; Gary and I sat together at the school dinner table and lunch was successfully added to afternoon attendance. This was maintained as over the next few days I phased out my presence so that I stood in the dining hall without sitting at table, and then Gary ate lunch without me being in the building at all. All this time, I continued the five minute routine (even if sometimes he ran out to the car after me asking if he could still come once the five minutes were up!), together with the Action Man game as we went into the building. Fun and the natural positives of school were eroding anxiety; in order to strengthen school attendance, tokens, praise and support were focussed on going to school rather than on anxiety and on not going. Progress was being made by both increasing the time of attendance and reducing the artificial anti-anxiety props. Gary was pleased and the school staff, although amused at my antics, had become increasingly supportive as Gary was seen to progress. His teacher soon took over the role of issuing Gary with his token at the end of each day — paving the way for my further withdrawal as the situation normalised. The other children had decided that I was probably a student teacher; they sought classroom help from me and accepted my particular involvement with Gary as some form of special tuition for a boy who had missed a lot of school.

At one point, the class teacher clearly saw me in this role and left me in charge of the class! As my presence was reduced, I was seen as less concerned with Gary alone, becoming rather like many of the parents dropping children off at school and collecting them at the end of the day.

Once over the school dinner barrier, I gave Gary increasing doses of school by taking him in slightly earlier each day. As Gary's school anxiety reduced further, he grew away from some of his props — he now joined in freely when the class was in the gym and went into the playground like everyone else.

Day twenty was a landmark. Gary attended the whole school day, and now I spent only a few minutes in the school's morning assembly to 'settle him in' before leaving him at school for the rest of the day. With the teacher issuing the end-of-day tokens, I arranged for Gary's mother to collect him on days 23 and 24, which went well. My sole remaining role in practice was winkling Gary out of the house by the five minute routine to take him to school each morning. My remaining therapeutic task was to wean Gary off the last of his artificial props — firstly, to phase out the token reinforcement and secondly, to phase out my presence and special routines in the morning.

The phasing out of morning routines neither succeeded nor went to plan. On day 26, I arranged for his mother to bring Gary to school and meet me there. This proved to be too disastrously big a step. Gary simply refused to enter school. Interestingly, early on the role of his mother had been to help inhibit anxiety; now her presence was clearly associated with, and actually triggered, all the old school avoidance behaviours that we had worked so hard and apparently so successfully to replace. To add to the problem, my attempts to train his mother to use the techniques I was using in the mornings (the obvious therapeutic step) had already failed. Day 27 underlined the problem, but at the expense of making his mother somewhat resentful. Gary refused to accompany his mother to school at all, but when after a time lapse I asked him to come using the usual routines, he did so without protest.

Trying to use a completely new means of journeying to school — changing the situation to a new and neutral one in which his mother might not trigger avoidance — I took Gary to school by bus. This tactic was wrecked by the dog Rex, which bounded on to the bus with us and snarled at the passengers until the driver stopped the bus and ordered me to take 'my' animal off! Of course, Gary was delighted at this situation and not at all anxious . . . however, I decided that it would be injudicious to repeat the exercise, as I had no way of stopping Rex from following us on what he clearly regarded as his walk to the bus stop. Practicalities erupt through the best laid plans.

It was all beginning to go wrong. Gary could attend school, but only if I took him. If he left home any morning with his mother, he refused to go to school. It was not practicable for him to go to school unaccompanied. Perhaps the journey in my car was too reinforcing — but no, he still came with me but not his mother on a non-car trip to school. Impasse.

We had to phase out special techniques, so I arranged for a colleague, whom Gary had not met, to take him to school instead of me for a while. My colleague was prepared to cope with any anxiety encountered, but would not be using my morning routines. He would simply drive Gary to school, thus phasing special procedures down to someone other than Gary's mother accompanying Gary to school. Gary accepted the lift to school, reported no anxiety, showed no reluctance, and attended the whole school day. It seemed that his mother was the critical factor: when she stayed at home, Gary now followed our new ABC behavioural sequence of willingly attending school with no further use for props such as me (or Action Man), but when she left the house with him the original problem ABC sequence immediately emerged.

I had two options. One was to accept the problem and arrange for Gary to be taken to school by someone other than his mother on a permanent basis. This had the advantage of being likely to achieve school attendance without anxiety. The second option was to arrange for his mother to accompany me in taking Gary to school every day, with the intention that her influence on Gary would become associated with going to school — and I could re-introduce previous procedures if necessary to ensure that Gary did keep attending with both of us. The risk in option two was that it might backfire, with Gary's mother's difficulties in taking him colouring and reducing my ability to get him there.

The choice was influenced by the fact that end of term was upon us, so I opted to arrange for somebody other than his mother to take Gary regularly to school. That Gary was now happy to attend school, provided that mother was not the one to take him, was underlined on the last day of term when Gary went to stay with a relative. The family had forgotten to tell me this, so it was very late when I arrived at the relative's house, not far from the school. I was pleasantly surprised to find that Gary had set off to school — late but entirely unaccompanied — and that he had arrived and stayed at school.

I had successfully reintroduced Gary to school over four and a half weeks and his anxiety had gone. Now he was kept there by the natural positives of school — such as meeting friends, enjoying at least some of the activities, and feeding the hamster — and was attending full days without the props of five minute routines, sweets, Action Man games or tokens that I had invented on ABC learning principles to channel his behaviour pattern along the chosen route. *But*, I had totally failed to 'generalise' this success by enabling his mother to take him to school without recurrence of the old problems. I assessed my efforts as largely successful but seriously undermined by this problem.

The next term, Gary was taken to school most (but for practical reasons, not all) days by a professional colleague who worked in the area — and as time passed (and Gary became more able to cross busy roads), Gary began to attend school every day unaccompanied on his own initiative. As often, time proved the solution. I no longer visited, but followed up Gary's progress by close contact with the school and was ready to re-introduce special procedures if this proved necessary. It did not. Ironically, Gary's school attendance record became and remained above average after treatment. His teacher also reported that he had settled well at school, and repeated use of the rating scales used in our initial assessment recorded much improvement in his general behaviour there.

As a final follow up check, an independent assessor evaluated Gary's progress 10 months later. He interviewed Gary, as well as his mother and headteacher. The latter confirmed that Gary remained a very regular attender at school, with very rare absences for illness only. Gary's overall behaviour was reported as still improved both at home and at school, and there was no evidence of any other problems emerging to take the place of school avoidance. Contrary to the worries of some people involved before treatment began, Gary had continued to attend school without continuation of any artificial rewards for doing so. This is usually the case — artificial reinforcers often become ignored once a new behaviour is established and are not needed as a permanent feature as sceptics usually anticipate. Notably, Gary had continued on his own to overcome the problem of going to school without his mother, and without any further special procedures. The overall picture was of a course of treatment that had achieved its goal of returning Gary to school without fear (although one can never be sure whether this was because the thinking behind the behavioural formulation and treatment was correct), but in which the final success of going to school without a third party taking him had actually been achieved by Gary *without* special procedures. Perhaps this can be explained by the continued effect of his new positive orientation towards school and its pay offs.

The independent evaluation did produce one key finding, which reveals a major issue in behaviour therapy. Gary's mother remained dissatisfied with my treatment, unlike Gary and the school. She accepted that he now went fearlessly to school, which was the whole object of the exercise, but she also felt that this had been too narrow a goal when she and the family had so many other problems of a non-behavioural nature. This is a salutary comment: behaviour therapy selects its goals and often achieves them and is therefore a valuable helping tool. Specific goals, however, are not the whole of a person, and the behavioural worker must acknowledge that he offers a specific service but in the context of possible needs for other more generalised help and advice such as social work advocacy and support — perhaps in areas such as housing and welfare difficulties.

Gary's treatment can perhaps be summed up as an effective treatment with some salutary warts on it.

Four

Tony
Bedtime Screaming

Tony's mother referred him because of her concern over his frequent tantrums and his habit on some nights of screaming continuously after going to bed. On such nights, she would put him to bed without any difficulty, but as soon as she had left him to go downstairs he would begin to scream — loudly. This would continue until she could stand it no more, when she would go back to Tony and bring him downstairs to calm him. After a time downstairs, he would go back to bed without further difficulty. She was worried that something might be going seriously wrong with Tony's development, and to compound the problem she and her husband could not agree over how to handle the situation. Her husband took the pragmatic line that since Tony stopped screaming as soon as he was brought downstairs again, he should be brought down whenever he screamed. Her own view was that the screaming would not happen if all was well with Tony. 'Giving in' to his screaming by bringing him down at night might encourage it, and could not be right since it had not stopped him screaming in the first place. She felt 'at her wits end'.

Tony was three years old — an age at which problems of behaviour, including bedtime problems and tantrums, are common enough to be regarded as normal. This can readily be established by consulting published surveys of the incidence of children's behaviour problems at various ages. Therefore, a clear decision had to be made in Tony's case, as in many others presenting problems which cannot be regarded as totally abnormal. Should the problems be labelled as such, and treatment or special management programmes be implemented, or should the parents simply be reassured that the behaviour problems they are experiencing are within the bounds of normal growing up?

Certainly there are cases where reassurance alone is the appropriate course of action. There are many parents who expect more of their children than is realistic for the child's age and many who specifically seek advice on whether a particular problem, although real enough, is something to worry about or not. Information drawn from incidence surveys can be the best response in many such cases, identifying those difficulties which are common passing phases.

Two things must nevertheless be said. Firstly, however common it may be, each problem does have to be handled in some way by parents, teachers and others. If, as in Tony's case, parents are unsure of what tactics to adopt and seek advice on the matter, clear advice should be offered if available to accompany whatever reassurances can be given. Reassuring someone that a genuine problem is nothing to worry about does not help them to handle it, and it is certainly possible to mishandle even a common difficulty. Secondly, the commonest problems can carry serious consequences for some individuals. A problem that can be carried by one family in its stride can break up relationships in another, and what one parent can accept as 'all part of growing up' can lead another to batter a child. If a parent asks for help, whatever it may be for, that request should be taken seriously.

Tony's parents were quite clear that they wanted help. However common tantrums and bedtime problems might be amongst three year olds, they wanted to know how to handle them in Tony. They were dogged by their sense of failure and frustration, and their lack of agreement over parental tactics so far. Tony's case was accepted for initial assessment to produce, if possible, clear and testable parenting tactics for his parents to follow.

At the first visit I met Tony briefly. He was a shy boy who mumbled 'Hello' and then retired to survey me suspiciously around the edge of an open door. Most of the session was spent trying to focus on various facts about the problems with his mother. Although Tony was the reason for the involvement, it seemed unlikely that I would be doing much direct work with him. Work on parenting tactics would involve mainly his mother and father. Whenever I visited I tried to adopt the role of 'friendly visitor' towards him. His father was usually out when I visited, although we made a point of meeting early on. He made it clear that now I was here he would follow my instructions with a healthy dose of scepticism, but he did not expect too much involvement. He would leave that to his wife as the parent with the prime responsibility for bringing up the child. Nevertheless he would at least give me and, whatever ideas I could come up with, a chance. I decided early on to focus my efforts on the mother. The textbooks say much about working with families as a whole, but this was the way that this family worked.

I had set myself three tasks for the initial assessment: to elicit from Tony's mother as detailed and objective a description of the tantrums and bedtime screaming as she could muster, to identify how these were handled at the moment, and to complete a standard questionnaire on problems of three-year-olds to gain an idea of Tony's overall adjustment. The main aim was, as it often has to be, to cut through generalised statements like 'he keeps having tantrums' to get at specifics such as the definition of a tantrum, the frequency with which the two problems occurred, the duration of screaming, and the events occurring before and after such occurrences.

The ABC model provided the guide to what needed to be sought — although it was not put to Tony's mother in such theoretical terms. ABC fitted Tony's problems particularly well since they were, fortunately, definable and easily recognised events with a clear beginning, middle and end. As usual, I found helpful the trick of asking Tony's mother to describe a tantrum and a screaming bout as if I were an actor and as if she were directing the scene on stage. Also as usual, the specific details that emerged clarified and changed the picture given by general statements like 'it's *always* happening, you know' — and thus avoided the dangers of my falling into easy but erroneous assumptions.

Tony's tantrums, his mother estimated, occurred two to three times a day on average and each lasted approximately 20 minutes. According to the 'actor's script' she described, Tony typically either refused to do something he was told to do — such as to put down a forkful of food he was brandishing — or he ignored a mild 'telling off' about some misdemeanour such as putting muddy shoes on the settee. When his mother repeated the instruction or the telling off more sternly, he began, as she put it, to escalate. He would begin to shout at her, then stamp his feet, scream and start to throw objects at her or across the room. From the examples given, mealtimes were clearly high risk occasions and it was often food, drink, crockery or cutlery that was hurled across the table. As often happens, asking the mother to describe the problem had immediately elicited the most dramatic event to have occurred in recent weeks and some time had to be spent teasing out more typical examples. A number of these were, however, produced once the dramatic ones were out of the way.

Turning to how these tantrums were handled exposed a classic parent's dilemma. Should the parent 'escalate' with the child, knowing that a tantrum with hurled objects would be the end product, or should one yield at some stage en route to the tantrum, thus avoiding the tantrum but at the cost of giving in to the child's refusal to cooperate? Neither option is very comfortable; one either generates a mountain out of what was all too often a molehill of an issue in the first place, or one lets the child win every time. Sometimes Tony's mother avoided tantrums by giving in — she said that although he had won, at least he was quiet about it. Sometimes, however, she decided that Tony could not be allowed to get away with or continue a particular misdeed, and then things ran to a tantrum. When she felt toughest, she removed him to his bedroom in the middle of a tantrum. This tactic usually cut the duration of the tantrum by about half.

Having explored the tantrum behaviour itself, together with its antecedents and consequences (the A, B and C of the analysis), we discussed the situations in which tantrums occurred, looking for factors tending to increase or decrease the likelihood of 'escalation'. This often yields a blank, but Tony's mother commented that tantrums most frequently occurred at home and had never been mentioned at Tony's playgroup. The presence of Tony's brother or sister — particularly when the family was collecting them from school — apparently increased the likelihood of tantrums, while the presence of his father seemed to reduce it.

It proved more difficult to secure an estimate of how many nights per week Tony's screaming occurred. His parents had simply not thought of it in numerical terms. It was certainly not every night, but was apparently often enough to constitute a major problem. Clearly, frequency needed to be determined by starting a baseline record. The 'actor's script' of a screaming episode was, however, almost a behaviour therapist's dream. Things occurred in the same sequence each time, there was no 'typical versus most dramatic' issue to sort out, and the description gave all the elements in the ABC analysis together with clues on what to do next.

His mother would tuck Tony up in bed and walk downstairs, leaving his door ajar. By the time she had reached the bottom of the stairs, he would have begun to call out. Moments later, his calls would warm up to repeated screams, seemingly only interrupted to take a breath and impossible to ignore even with the television on and the door closed. How long this stage continued depended on the debate between Tony's parents on what to do next. Eventually one or the other parent would go to Tony and carry him downstairs. As soon as he was picked up, he would stop screaming. He would enjoy a cup of cocoa and a cuddle on Mum or Dad's lap in front of the television, and then return to bed as good as gold.

The final stage of the first visit was to complete a standard behavioural questionnaire about aspects of Tony's behaviour and development other than our 'target' problems. Analysing the answers back at the office, I found Tony's scores to be within the normal range. There was no evidence here of any wider or other form of psychological disorder. Before my second visit to the family, Tony was taken to his family doctor for a thorough check-up to exclude any physical problems. The report was clear.

The next step was to formulate a possible explanation of what might be maintaining Tony's problems, in a way which would lead to a plan of action. As usual the treatment plan needed to carry a clear prediction of what changes would result, so that the whole formulation of explanation and treatment plan could be assessed as helpful or useless in practice, according to whether or not the predicted changes actually occurred.

The nocturnal screaming had emerged as the most worrying problem, as well as technically the most straightforward, so we started the behavioural formulation there. Using the ABC model, the B (behaviour) was now well defined, although it needed baseline recording to establish frequency. The A (antecedent) event was clear — being left at bedtime. However, this did not take us much further since no triggering factors or events seemed to predict that screaming would occur one bedtime and not another. His father's presence or that of the other children, which influenced tantrums, did not influence screaming. The C (consequences) element was, however, the likely key to helping Tony and his parents. After being left to scream for a variable period of time, Tony was brought downstairs for a cuddle, a cup of cocoa, and a brief spell of television. Even more significant, he inevitably stopped screaming the second he was picked up, for which his parents were understandably grateful.

Cuddles, cocoa and television are all likely to be pleasant, so screaming was being followed by rewarding consequences. Could it be that Tony's parents were simply reinforcing the screaming and so maintaining the problem? More subtly, Tony *stopping* screaming was a pleasant consequence for his parents' carrying him out of bed. Were they being reinforced for 'bringing him down' by the fact that it stopped the screams? The cessation of something unpleasant — like hearing a child scream — can be just as pleasant and reinforcing as a 'straight' pleasant consequence. A vicious circle seemed a distinct possibility. The obvious move was to try to remove the positive consequences that might be reinforcing and thus strengthening and prolonging the screaming.

Converting this to a practicable treatment strategy, I asked Tony's parents to put him to bed and come downstairs as usual each night. When he began screaming, they were simply to check that there was no unusual cause and then to come downstairs. They were *not* to bring him down. Specifically, this should stop the possibly reinforcing consequences of cuddles, cocoa and television as pay offs for screaming. If the assessment was right, we would predict that at first Tony's screaming would increase, but that it would then gradually disappear. This prediction came from the published accounts of this 'removing the reinforcement' strategy (termed inelegantly the 'extinction' of a problem in the jargon). If this did not happen, we would have to reassess the problem and our strategy. I asked the parents to increase the attention they gave Tony during the day, so that he was compensated for loss of attention at night.

Being left upstairs was not new to Tony; it was one of the approaches his parents had already tried from time to time. Now, however, it was to be used consistently and his parents were to monitor its effectiveness by timing his screaming each night. We were focussing on just one tactic for a while and concentrating its consistency. His father did say 'we've tried all that' — but accepted that he had never separated it out from a conflicting mixture of other approaches and that therefore he had never tested its effects properly. Furthermore, he saw some common sense logic to the reasons for picking this tactic from all the others he had tried.

We decided to approach the temper tantrums with another 'removing the reinforcement' tactic, although I was on less firm ground here since I could not identify so easily the probable reinforcing 'pay offs'. Under these circumstances, instead of removing the reinforcers from the child, one can remove the child from the possible reinforcers. Thus I asked Tony's parents to remove him from the room for five minutes every time that he developed a full tantrum. Putting him in his bedroom worked in practice when we tried it: he stayed there until brought back downstairs, he did not object once the tantrum began to subside, and the five minute period was usually long enough for the tantrum to subside without Tony either objecting to a long period 'out' or becoming involved in any new activity in his room. If he had done that, it could have become a new reinforcer for tantrums and given our treatment a reverse effect. The theory was that this 'time out' from reinforcement would break the link between tantrums and whatever the reinforcing consequences were — at various times, getting his own way by a tantrum, the disruption of a situation, or perhaps the giggles of his siblings. The prediction was that tantrums would reduce in frequency with this time out procedure.

Although removing Tony may seem harsh, it must be noted that this was again no more than concentrating on one of the tactics his parents had already been using, while at the same time cutting out the competing tactics and monitoring the results of the now isolated tactic by meticulous record-keeping. In terms of possible distress to a child, it is also often the case that 'five minutes out' immediately contingent upon the occurrence of the problem behaviour is not only more effective, but also less distressing than a parent escalating into a major punishment.

From the child's point of view, five minutes in his bedroom is arguably preferable to being sent to bed early, being deprived of privileges, being smacked, or a parent losing his or her temper.

Before starting treatment, Tony's parents should have been asked to keep the baseline record of his screaming and tantrums on a specially designed chart, with which we could compare future records to assess progress. Normally, one aims to secure a baseline record early in assessment, so that it gives a clear pre-treatment position statement before any changes take place. Only with such a clear baseline can one measure subsequent changes (good or bad) with any confidence, or be sure that any changes only began as treatment was introduced.

In this case, as sometimes happens in practice, we lost our opportunity to gather baseline data. With it we also lost some of the evaluative element of a behavioural treatment. Before I had even seen Tony's parents, other people had outlined the type of approach I was likely to adopt. Not unreasonably, the parents had asked this when the referral was first suggested to them. They were already changing tactics before we could discuss a baseline. To request continuation of the previous handling and inconsistency was clearly unrealistic. Furthermore, there was the danger of premature and piecemeal implementation of treatment since the treatment strategies we were discussing were essentially concentrated versions of some of the tactics already in use. I had to accept that treatment advice had to be given straight away, accept the lost baseline with good grace, but insist on good treatment records from the start. Luckily, Tony's mother enjoyed record-keeping and kept charts consistently up to date. A therapist is not always so lucky.

One chart recorded the occurrence of each daytime tantrum, with a brief 'actor's script' description. On the other, bedtime tantrums were to be entered, together with the duration of each one. Leaving instructions to begin the 'time out' routine for all tantrums, and to stop bringing Tony downstairs for screaming, I left the house with a promise to return at the end of the week. As always on initiating a treatment, there was the niggling feeling that one's predictions of the changes to come sounded rather less than convincing and that Tony might prove immune to such simple influences, or do something completely unexpected.

In his first week, Tony only had one tantrum and one evening of bedtime screaming. The tantrum had stopped within the first two minutes of his five minute time out. On the other hand, the screaming had continued for almost half and hour. The low frequency led us to bemoan the lack of a baseline for comparison, although Tony's mother said how pleased she was with what she stated was a reduction. Tony's

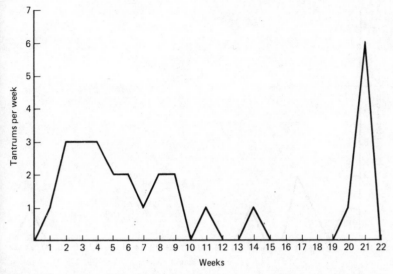

Fig. 4 Frequency of Tony's tantrums.

record of tantrums (see Fig. 4) showed a rise to three tantrums the following week — apparently more typical, but still far less than one would have expected from previous reports of Tony's behaviour. Record charts are the vital spouse of treatment, and here they showed that we were really offering parenting tactics rather than treating frequent abnormal behaviour. We discussed the recorded frequency, agreed that the tactics remained appropriate, and so continued. It is worth noting that records often show a very different picture to the general view that was held before they were started: this is one good reason for insisting that they be kept.

Figure 5 shows Tony's bedtime screaming during my involvement with him. The duration ranged from five to thirty minutes of continuous screaming. Tony was left in his room on each occasion except the second, when his mother was out for the evening and his father, preoccupied with other things, had forgotten about the new rules and had brought him downstairs. In theory, if repeated this could lead to the reversed treatment effect of strengthening the screaming problem, since *occasional* reinforcement of an action by pleasant consequences is a good way of ensuring its future repetition. Indeed, such 'partial reinforcement' is used in some treatment programmes to bolster a newly learned action against the very extinction that we were hoping for with Tony's screaming. The theory, substantiated by numerous experiments, is that one learns to keep on producing an action if it only

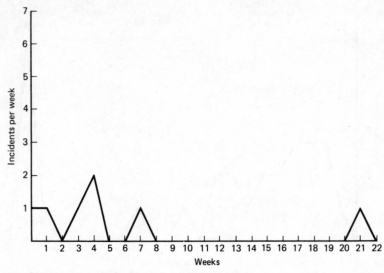

Fig. 5 Frequency of Tony's night-time screaming.

occasionally earns a pay off. In comparison, an action which earns a pay off every time is learned quickly but less securely — so that it is soon lost if the pay offs cease. The trite but memorable example is that people will work one-armed bandit machines hard and long for an occasional pay off, but soon give up use of a coffee machine if it stops reinforcing their actions with cups of coffee. In treatment programmes, frequent reinforcement is commonly used to gain rapid early learning, followed by partial reinforcement to keep the learned actions in use when the pay offs become infrequent.

In Tony's case, we discussed the dangers of reversing the treatment effect by occasionally reinforcing screaming, but once was not enough to damage progress. The simplest of treatment tactics are often not followed consistently, and therefore records usually show not the changes associated with the planned treatment programme, but with some variant of it. One must check closely on some programmes because although simple, they represent two-edged swords whose effects can swing into reverse.

Tony's treatment records in Figs. 4 and 5 show that the predicted rise in his bedtime screaming did occur, followed by the hoped-for dropping away — to zero after eight weeks of the non-reinforcement tactic. What was not expected was the sustained rise in tantrums which, although objectively never highly frequent, nevertheless took fifteen weeks to drop to zero. Time out should have been the quicker-acting of the two tactics; for Tony, the expected simply did not prove to be the case in practice. Throughout the initial treatment period, Tony's records showed only five incidents of bedtime screaming, but 21 daytime tantrums. The tantrums in weeks 11 and 14 were, however, described as less severe than usual. The 'actor's script' summaries showed that most tantrums occurred at mealtimes, and typical occurrences involved throwing milk or cutlery across the table.

It is wise to keep a check on critical aspects of any treatment, and on any possible side-effects, in addition to one's main treatment records. One concern with Tony was the possibility that he might find time out in his bedroom more unpleasant than we had intended, or even that it might create an aversion to his bedroom. His parents were questioned on these issues early in treatment and again later as changes began to occur. Tony was not reported as showing signs of distress on his way to or while in his room. He appeared to accept it as simply a predictable and familiar routine which occurred immediately that he had a tantrum. Consistently, his tantrums subsided quickly once he had been taken from the room. However, one problem did appear during treatment; Tony, who had recently become dry at night, suffered a brief recurrence of bedwetting. This, however, stopped again entirely on its own, and in a child of only three was thus considered likely to be a 'normal lapse' rather than a developing side-effect of treatment.

We decided to phase treatment out from week 11 — although in practice it phased itself out as the problems which triggered the special parenting tactics faded out. After problem behaviours have 'extinguished' themselves following the removal of the reinforcing pay offs that had maintained them, theory predicts their brief recurrence after a problem-free period. We were all pleased with progress so far, but kept the record charts in use, and settled down to wait for a return of Tony's problems.

They started again with a vengeance in week 20. After five tantrum-free weeks, Tony threw his entire dinner and a cup of hot cocoa across the table. At the same time he began to be generally aggressive. He also soiled his pants in the same week. The following week, after 12 weeks without any bedtime screaming, this problem returned as well. For these two weeks, Tony's problems became worse than they had been when we started. The recurrences arose immediately after a weekend visit by relatives, although the coincidence in time may have been no more than a coincidence. As had been agreed with his parents, Tony's difficulties were handled in exactly the same was as before, and both problems disappeared again (as did the aggression) within two weeks. The soiling did not happen a second time and the bedwetting did not recur.

We now considered our work with Tony and his family to be complete other than the routine follow up enquiries to check that all remained well. The problems that Tony's parents had sought help in handling were gone. Furthermore, they had acquired a way of reacting effectively to these problems should they recur. Even Tony's father was pleased.

Ten weeks later it happened. Bedtime screaming recurred a second time. This time, Tony also added a completely new problem. On three occasions in one week, when his mother asked him to do something, he reacted by repetitively screaming her Christian name. Now, one of the major predictions made by oppenents of behavioural treatment is that eliminating one problem will run the risk of some presumed underlying disturbance emerging in a new form through a substitute symptom. Behaviour therapists counter this by pointing out that symptom substitution had not been found to follow behavioural treatments in practice. Yet here was Tony demonstrating exactly what shouldn't happen. Had I simply converted Tony's tantrums into name-screaming sessions?

As if to underline my fears that I had done Tony a disservice rather than helping the family to cope, the next two weeks were marked by a rising number of tantrums (five in the second week) and no screaming, either of names or at bedtime. He seemed to be screaming *or* having tantrums, as interchangeable sets of problems. To make matters worse, neither I nor his parents could identify any possible factors or changes at home which might have precipitated his relapse. Textbook cases do not end up like this, and an eminent visiting professor to whom I described Tony commented, something short of helpfully, 'Oh dear, that shouldn't have happened, should it?'

Tony's parents followed our standing agreement over parenting tactics, and used time out for the renewed tantrums together with the usual avoidance of pay offs for nocturnal screaming. His mother was extremely upset at his name-screaming, particularly as it occurred in public while on the way home from collecting the older children from school. It seemed a public confirmation of all her difficulties. Something had to be done about the name-screaming, and we decided jointly to analyse this new problem behaviourally as we had the other two. To give up through theoretical fears of symptom substitution did not seem practicable just then: Tony's mother had to work out some way of reacting to the renewed problems, behavioural tactics had produced at least some change in the past, and we could not leave Tony worse off than before we had started.

We covered some very familiar ground when we analysed the name-screaming. Whenever Tony screamed her name, his mother would try to ignore it but usually gave in and let him have his own way. Logically, pay offs similar to those involved in nocturnal screaming could be suspected of reinforcing name-screaming. Additionally, Tony's mother's pay off for giving in was immediate relief from the screaming, and dangerously, the fact that screaming did not *always* produce pay offs (sometimes there were no other people to hear and mother could hold out) created the partial reinforcement situation likely to maintain the problem over a long period. We concluded that name-screaming, like Tony's other problems, was probably being maintained by attention.

We added an 'ignore name-screaming' rule to our parenting tactics. Although this exposed Tony's mother to some public embarrassment, she said that she did not mind this since we had selected a tactic she knew had worked with Tony before. At the same time we reviewed all our other decisions on ways of responding to Tony's behaviour. A stark mistake emerged.

The pay offs for screaming and tantrums that we had been cutting out all involved parental attention, but it was the *link* between attention and problems we wanted to reduce, not the overall amount of attention that Tony received from his parents. Early on, I had asked that Tony should be given extra attention at problem-free times during the day, to compensate for any loss of attention and parental contact through time out and loss of evening sessions downstairs. However, I had failed to schedule this extra attention in with proper treatment instructions. I had left it as a general exhortation and not kept any record of its implementation. It transpired that Tony's parents had not increased daytime attention, but had followed the natural but unfortunate and all-too-common tendency to leave the boy well alone while he was being good 'in case they set him off again'. Treatments, such as time out and problem extinction which reduce reinforcement, need to be accompanied by a transfer of reinforcement to desirable alternative behaviour. One cannot expect success by trying to reduce problem behaviours and leaving a vacuum in their place.

We now viewed Tony's name-screaming not as an example of symptom substitution (with all its attendant assumptions of problems as 'safety-valves' for underlying disturbance), but as the predictable result of a faulty behavioural programme. Having once lost tantrums and nocturnal screaming as routes to attention, it was not surprising that any alternative route to the same pay off should escalate quickly. The programme fault was in failing to establish normal behaviour as the route to extra replacement attention, thus leaving to random selection the development of the alternative route. We had missed our opportunity to choose a new route to attention for Tony. This was now rectified by scheduling set occasions for him to be given extra personal attention at problem-free times, including cuddles and individual contact with one parent.

The treatment prediction was now that the removal of pay offs for Tony's three problems should lead to their temporary increase and then elimination, while the transfer of attention to a range of acceptable activities should forestall the emergence of new alternative problems. The record of problems at this stage of Tony's treatment is reproduced in Fig. 6. All three problems ceased completely in six weeks, and this time no new alternatives were reported. It was reassuring that Tony's tantrums and screaming did not continue as alternatives, but occurred together in weeks four to six. This was more consistent with the temporary rise predicted for a non-reinforcement behavioural treatment than with any idea of symptom substitution. Substitute symptoms of something underlying should not occur together, and if they can all be made to disappear at the same time, they cannot be substitute symptoms.

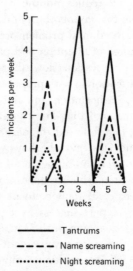

Fig. 6 Recurrence of Tony's problems.

To check for any further relapses or side effects, I followed up Tony's progress for a year. He remained free of his original problems and of any new problems.

My involvement with Tony and his parents had at times been

nerve-wracking — but together we had worked out practical parenting tactics to replace uncertainty and inconsistency, and Tony entered school a straightforward little boy. There was nothing novel in his treatment, but it represented some classic elements of behavioural work with children: we had analysed the learning influences in his parenting to focus common sense consistently on problems of concern, and we had used objective treatment records to guide what we were doing. In theory, it was all very simple.

Five

Lynne
Paired Reading

I and many colleagues have long had a professional interest in the development of straightforward and largely common sense techniques that parents can use with their children at home. Professionals can become extremely sophisticated in the processes of assessment and special treatments, but all professionals working with children's problems spend a vast proportion of their time giving what might be termed simply 'advice to parents'. It is the parents and not the professionals who live with the children in most cases, and it is the parents who have to balance time spent on special measures with the constraints of home and family — the constraints of jobs, the limited time left after the tasks of daily survival have been completed, the other children, the housing problems, and the financial stress. Often nowadays all these responsibilities have to be managed by a single parent. Therefore therapeutic 'things for parents to do' must realistically satisfy a 'cost effective' criterion in terms of good returns for an input that can be managed realistically at home. Home-use techniques must also be robust in the sense that they must work despite the inevitable mistakes and inconsistencies in their use. They are not put into practice by hard pressed parents in precisely the pristine form in which they may be described in journal articles. A procedure for home-use needs to be: (1) simple, (2) seen to be logical and based on acceptable common sense, (3) easily taught in a short period of time, and (4) readily sustainable over a period of time at home without the need for intensive professional supervision.

Reading problems present an area that calls for a home-use technique that fits these criteria, and 'paired reading' represents my own attempt to design such a technique. Lynne's use of the technique typifies its use with many children in the UK and elsewhere.

My first contact with Lynne was through the headmaster of her primary school, who had identified her as a child with a clear problem in reading but within the normal range of intelligence (this had been tested in the recent past). The headmaster was also keen to develop parent-used reading techniques for home use, because he had recently lost his remedial reading staff in a round of staffing reductions and was feeling increasingly reliant on self-help techniques to back up normal class teaching. Already he had brought a number of mothers in to school during the school day to help the poor readers.

I met Lynne and her mother at a specially arranged session after school, in one of those general purpose corners that most schools seem to have and that store parts of old reading schemes, musical instruments, lost clothing, paper guillotines and fossilised whale teeth — as well as serving as a base for visitors like psychologists and students doing special projects with children. Such sessions always begin in an informal atmosphere because usually the first task is to find some adult-sized chairs, poached from elsewhere.

Lynne was eleven and a half, and her mother felt her reading had become a major problem. Lynne's view of reading was becoming prejudiced by her increasing failure at it. She was beginning to avoid reading whenever possible and in so doing, was avoiding much of the school work that involved reading. Like so many children with reading problems, she was fast becoming anti-school. The last thing to interest her would be the idea of extra reading at home. She presented the typical challenge of the poor reader — the need to be motivated. Something needed to imbue boring black print with an element of fun.

I arranged two evening sessions with Lynne and her mother in the first week, each three quarters of an hour long. The first was for assessment and the second for 'paired reading' training, assuming that this was appropriate after the assessment. A shorter check-up session was arranged for week two and then for each fortnight after that, with a final session of half an hour after 12 weeks to assess progress. Lynne and her mother (her mother predictably more enthusiastic than Lynne — 'you must, love . . . you *know* you need help with your reading') had agreed to spend a quarter of an hour every day at home on reading. The pattern was a standard one and fairly well tried; past experience was that the vast majority of parents and children can learn 'paired reading' to home-use standard within three quarters of an hour, and fortnightly check-up sessions normally last only ten minutes to clear minor problems and correct slight drifting from routines. I find that a fortnight is a key length of time for many home-based techniques with children, from using enuresis alarms, to token systems, to paired reading. It appears to be an optimum time, at least in my own practice, between professional contacts; parents and children can sustain procedures with only minor, easily corrected drifts, for two weeks, but if left unsupported for longer seem to run into an accelerating deviation or breakdown from what was intended. (Of course, this is only an hypothesis generated from experience — but it is testable!)

Lynne's first assessment visit contained two elements. First, I asked her mother to wait outside in the hall while I administered the Neale Analysis of Reading Ability to Lynne. This is a standardised reading test — that is, the reading scores found when a large 'standardisation sample' of children were given this test allow the normal scores for children of different ages to be identified. In turn this means that any score by a child being tested can be turned into a 'reading age', using tables of scores and ages printed in the manual. I tested Lynne on her own, because it can be distracting to test with a parent next to the child — the tester has to try to ignore the parent and the child should not be able to seek or receive their parent's help. To be valid, testing has to be kept standard; the instructions, comments and reactions to be given by the tester are formally laid down in the test manual. Inappropriate help or comment can invalidate the test.

Lynne read the first, simple story in the Neale book to me. I recorded her errors under various categories and gave her the words she could not manage within the stipulated four seconds. On the second story (the test has a series of one page stories of increasing difficulty) we began to run into trouble, with wild guesses, complete halts despite efforts at 'sound building', and smaller words left out completely. I stopped testing when Lynne reached the standard 'ceiling' number of errors in a single passage. After each story, she was asked simple comprehension questions. The Neale gives three reading ages — for accuracy (the most useful), for comprehension (less useful — not surprisingly, low accuracy leads to low comprehension, but it is important to know if the two are very dissimilar), and for speed of reading (I rarely find this useful). Lynne's reading age for accuracy was 8 years 10 months and her age for comprehension was 10 years 8 months. With her chronological age of 11 years 6 months, she was 2 years 8 months behind in her reading accuracy.

I confirmed with her mother that the test showed that Lynne was sufficiently behind in reading to merit special attention. I also assured Lynne that the worst was now over and the next session would become interesting and fun. She looked decidedly sceptical. On this assessment Lynne appeared a good candidate for paired reading: her reading was behind, but included basic phonetic skills in building sounds into words; she could read simple words, but her reading often fell to pieces when the passage became tough, with loss of even the small words that she could normally manage; she did not enjoy reading, lacked confidence in anything to do with reading, and was increasingly resistant to simplified books such as reading scheme books that she knew were meant for a lower class.

The second element of the session was simply to ask Lynne and her mother to show me what they normally did to help with reading at home — which they said they did 'sometimes, when we can manage to fit it in'.

I had asked them to bring a suitable book with them, and Lynne and her mother sat next to each other across the table with the book between them. Lynne began to read, hesitantly but with few problems — it was a very simple book. Her mother listened to her quietly. When Lynne made a mistake or became stuck, her mother either corrected her or said something along the following lines: 'Come on, Lynne. You got that word on the other page. Try and have another go.'

This performance is typical of parents (and often teachers) 'hearing children read'. And that is precisely what usually happens — the adult listens. However, learning principles would suggest that this common practice is likely to produce a very low yield in increased reading performance. The adult is sitting in total silence when the child is reading correctly. Silence is not very reinforcing of correct reading. The child is receiving less reinforcement for reading correctly than she does during a conversation with her mother, when her words can be seen to produce eye contact, nods, smiles and sounds of approval. I find that listening in silence and making no eye contact or sounds or gestures of approval or of acknowledgement is a very effective way of extinguishing unwanted conversations. Try it on an uninvited salesman — but do not expect it to encourage correct reading.

Observing Lynne across the table, one could see that many problem words were spoken questioningly rather than definitely — as if she were seeking confirmation that her unsure attempt was right. She even looked up at her mother for some sign at some of these points — but received nothing. Try observing an adult 'hearing a child read' and watch for positive reactions to correct reading, including praise, sounds ('uh-huh', 'mm') or approving physical contacts. Listen when the child makes unsure pronunciations with a questioning intonation and note what proportion receive a confirming response. Usually the only responses that the child does receive are negative reactions to errors. Even though the parent or teacher means to encourage the child, it is probably anxiety-provoking to say 'come on, try it again. You got it on the other page', when clearly the child hasn't 'got it' on this page. A reading session, whether at home or school, which contains more aversive or anxiety-provoking than praising adult reactions is ill advised — it is punishing rather than reinforcing reading.

When I asked her, Lynne's mother assured me that she believed in encouraging Lynne when she managed to read correctly. While I explained what I had just observed in terms of the balance of positive and negative reactions, she nodded and made sounds of agreement. Whenever I stopped and raised a quizzical eyebrow, she quickly made an agreeing noise. She was embarrassed when I pointed out that she had just given me more positive feedback for my standard patter than she had been giving Lynne for getting her words right. The point went home, and we agreed that the first task for our next session together would be to practise increasing the positive feedback to Lynne for getting words right — a basic of paired reading and a very simple derivation from research-based learning principles. I finished by promising Lynne that from now on what we were going to do really would be fun. Perhaps from what we had just done, she realised that Mum and not just she had some learning to do. In any case she looked less sceptical.

Between sessions one and two, I ran a tape recording that I had made of Lynne and her mother working on reading before any 'paired reading' training. Having noted the (minimal) number of positive responses by mother, I could calculate a baseline reinforcement rate. This showed that only 2% of words correctly read were being reinforced.

Later in the week, we met again for session two — the 'paired reading' training session. I had asked Lynne to bring a book again, but this time one she wanted to read but found difficult. I wanted the book to be suited to her interests and *chronological* age, rather than reading age.

We began with training in giving reinforcement of correct reading. I asked Lynne to read to me from her book and assured her that she would be told any word that she could not manage. Lynne did manage the first sentence and a half without mishap, while I kept up a continuous feedback of positive words 'good . . . yes . . . correct . . . that's it, well done Lynne . . . good'. Any word intoned as a question or with uncertainty was given immediate approval if right. I gave Lynne the correct answer for any word she could not manage on her own.

Lynne's mother then tried the same. She produced very few reinforcing words, and Lynne had become stuck before receiving any positive feedback for what she had already read correctly. Discussing the exercise afterwards, her mother said that keeping up a patter of reinforcement felt extremely awkward and made her feel embarrassed. Furthermore, she was worried that it would distract Lynne. Asked directly, however, Lynne stated that she liked the feedback to tell her when she was getting things right and did not find it at all off-putting. These comments are almost universal at the start of 'paired reading'; most parents think reinforcement awkward and distracting, most children like it.

However at this point, I must admit that a few years ago, one boy stopped me during a demonstration of reinforcement for correct reading, and said 'I wish you'd stop saying "Good boy" — I'm not a dog'. While he read on, I sat for a while in silence, wondering what the good behaviour therapist should do under these circumstances and licking my wounds. Some sentences later, he stopped again and said 'But please say when its correct'. So I restarted my feedback . . . 'Correct . . . yes . . . correct'. One child's reinforcement may be another's poison!

Lynne's mother tried again, with instructions to keep the reinforcing feedback to a high enough level to feel self-conscious doing it. She was to 'seal in' Lynne's correct reading performance by making sure that Lynne could never be in any doubt that she had read the last word correctly. With me prompting across the table (and reinforcing Mum for reinforcing Lynne!), we managed to increase the proportion of words reinforced (according to the tape) to 50%; a 25-fold increase. The best achieved on a tape during the tuition period was 75%. There was some dropping off later, but the level remained consistently and markedly higher than baseline, demonstrating a clear input of reinforcement for correct reading. At subsequent sessions, Lynne's mother commented that reinforcement was coming more naturally. She was beginning to use 'mm-huh' as her normal feedback — it was the way she acknowledged what was said to her in normal conversation and so fitted the bill well. Whether the net result of the various elements of tuition, including reinforcement, was a measurable improvement in reading would have to wait to be seen by the post test.

Having practised her mother's reinforcement of Lynne's correct reading, we moved on to the second component of 'paired reading'. This is simultaneous reading by parent and child — reading out loud together from the chosen book. In effect this is reading a duet. The parent should signal the start of reading together by pointing to the first word, and should control the pace, if necessary, by continuing to point to each syllable as it is to be said. This pace needs to be adjusted by the parent to find the speed best suited to the child — if the pace is too fast, the child will miss out words or syllables, skipping to keep up. If too slow, the child will overtake the parent.

Simultaneous reading places a great load on the parent's reading capacity, and it is important to check that the selected parent can cope and is a competent reader. It is possible for a parent with reading problems to tutor a child with reading problems (or even for an older child to tutor a younger one), provided that the parent's reading ability is substantially ahead of the child's. Reading problems do tend to run in some families, and one must change strategy if the parent's reading age is too close to the child's. Usually it is the mother who arrives to work with the child, but in a significant minority of my 'paired reading' cases a father with a higher reading age has taken over — usually without any ill-feelings and often already trained in 'paired reading' by the child before arriving for Dad's official training session with me.

I demonstrated simultaneous reading with Lynne, starting us off by putting my finger down above the first word and pointing to each syllable as we went on. Like many children starting 'paired reading', Lynne found it easier than expected and soon we caught on to each other's reading pace and style (none of the difficulty I encountered once when trying to help a tutor with a strong Irish brogue trying to read simultaneously with a boy who spoke in extreme Birmingham!). However, she did stop reading when we hit a particularly difficult word — waiting to hear me read it first. The idea of simultaneous reading is that the child is learning words by moulding her version to the 'model' version provided by a tutor reading the same word at the same time. The tutor's voice is an ever present guide through the maze of words. This learning process is a variation on the theme of 'participant modelling' (see Chapter 1).

However, the system breaks down if the child simply stops at a difficult word, thus missing any learning effect of moulding her version to a simultaneous model. I told Lynne that she should think of our reading together as me giving her a piggy back over the difficult words — as long as she held on and let me carry her through she would be alright. Whatever she did, though, she should not jump off the ride whenever I was about to carry her over a problem.

To make the point, I asked Lynne to look down the page until she spotted a word she could not possibly read. She picked the word 'conjuror'. I showed the word to her mother. Telling her to keep reading at all costs when she reached it, even if all she thought she could do was to make a noise like one does when pretending to sing along with a song that one doesn't know, we set off through the sentence towards 'conjuror'. We plodded steadily through the syllables, up to 'conjuror' through 'conjuror', and out the other side of 'conjuror' on to the full stop.

Lynne's mother agreed that Lynne's version of the word had been passably close to 'conjuror' and was recognisable as such. Lynne nodded and grinned when I asked her if she now believed I could piggy back her through nasty words if only we both kept going. A few minutes later we checked that Lynne could still remember 'conjuror' on her own. She could. It is an effective demonstration that very frequently works first time.

Next it was her mother's turn to try simultaneous reading. Lynne went round to her mother's side of the table with her book and they set off reading together. Five words later they ground to a halt in confusion, each reading a different word. 'Paired reading' is more difficult than it looks, but fortunately the techniques can be learnt in a short space of time.

If Lynne could learn words by moulding her efforts to an adult's model, then why should her mother not learn how to do 'paired reading' by moulding her technique to a model supplied by me? We tried this; I read simultaneously with Lynne *and* her mother. I stood behind Lynne and her mother and all three of us read a page simultaneously together — including another 'conjuror'. Then I faded out once we were well established on a steady pace, leaving Lynne's mother continuing satisfactorily with her daughter. Things were going well. Mother was beginning to adjust the pace as needed while still keeping control, and their reading sounded right; somewhat slower than speech, with a steady pacing of the syllables — almost as if they were reading to a metronome.

After twenty minutes of the session, Lynne and her mother could read together passably well, and the mother could produce a much increased level of positive feedback (or praise, or reinforcement, whichever one prefers to call it) for Lynne's correct solo reading. Now it was time to put the two 'paired reading' components (reinforced individual reading and simultaneous reading) together.

I explained to Lynne that the two types of reading were rather like two gears, the individual gear and the simultaneous gear, and that there were specific ways of changing from one to the other and back again. Lynne and her mother should always start by reading simultaneously. Lynne was to have control over the change to individual reading: when she felt able to read alone, even if only for a word or two, she was to knock on the table. We practised this. We agreed that a knock on the table was the right sort of signal because it did not interrupt what one was saying while reading. As soon as she knocked, Mum was to stop reading with her, allowing Lynne to carry on reading alone — but remembering to switch from reading with her to giving plenty of praise as long as Lynne was managing the words correctly. If Lynne made an error, her mother should point it out (perhaps with her thumb stopped above the word) to let Lynne try it a second time. However if she could not manage the word within a count of four seconds (counted silently by her mother), she was to be given the word and they were then to say it simultaneously. Giving the answer and saying the problem word together (to learn it by the moulding process) was always to be the change of gear back to simultaneous reading, which should continue until Lynne knocked again.

I demonstrated this with Lynne, who picked up the routine well, although I had to prompt her to knock. 'Paired reading' is designed to be easily adopted by the child; remembering the technique is very much in the parent's court. When her mother tried the full routine with Lynne, they both ground to a confused halt on four occasions before they managed to keep going on the right track, with me prompting from across the table. Lynne's mother fell into the usual fault of forgetting to praise Lynne at all while she was reading alone, and Lynne showed the usual initial reluctance to knock. I thus adopted my usual tactics of competing with the mother in praising the child to encourage positive feedback, and of tapping Lynne's hand from time to time to encourage her to knock. Lynne's mother felt like a learner car driver: she knew all the steps to take, but the actions seemed to come together too quickly and got out of sequence with disastrous, although often by now amusing results. Good: mum and child were smiling, and learning to read this way was becoming fun.

By the end of the session, we had achieved 'paired reading' by Lynne and her mother. The technique had been mastered initially in practice. We now summarised it to help commit it to memory for home-use: always start in Together Gear — reading from the book simultaneously, the mother's finger controlling the pace, keeping going through problem words and going back to do the word together again if one of them stopped. Lynne knocks to change to Solo Gear in which she reads aloud alone, the mother giving plenty of praise, pointing out mistakes with her thumb and giving the word if Lynne is still stuck after four seconds. If a word is given, change back to Together Gear by saying the problem word together and continuing together until another knock. In learning terms, reading together should teach Lynne words by moulding her efforts to the parent's model, praise during solo reading should reinforce and strengthen her correct reading, and limiting any struggles on problem words to four seconds should avoid the punishing and learning-destructive anxiety of unsuccessful striving.

I sent the family away with a diary chart to record home 'paired reading' sessions, and asked Lynne and her mother to do a quarter of an hour's 'paired reading' every evening. As Lynne went to the door, I

said 'one question before you escape, Lynne. Is paired reading fun?'
'Yes', she said 'it's better than I thought it would be.'

*   *   *

A week later, we were together again for our first check-up session.
First we reviewed the record chart of sessions held at home. Of a
possible seven sessions, Lynne and her mother had managed five;
family crises and practicalities had prevented the other two. This is a
fairly typical record; I think it is more important to maintain consistency and continuation of technique than 100% application. The greater
danger lies in procedures petering out, losing the competition with
Guide meetings, ballet lessons, television and tiredness, rather than in
a low but steady level of missed sessions. One problem with Lynne was
competition with a particular television programme. I suggested that
the 'paired reading' session should begin if possible 20 minutes before
the programme, so that the programme might reinforce the session
(after a five minute gap to prevent too much clock-watching). There
were no other problems, and both said they were enjoying 'paired
reading'. Lynne found it all fun and therefore attractive and motivat-
ing. In addition she was enjoying her book, the 'oldest' age group book
she had read. Her mother found it helpful to have a clear (and she
thought enjoyable) technique to follow — helping Lynne read this way
was a pleasant mother and daughter experience rather than a frustrating
one leading to rows and resentment. There is probably a 'placebo'
effect in this positive parental attention which contributes to learning to
read — one researcher who worked with 'paired reading' called this the
'Mum effect'. I hope soon to test this hypothesis in practice, by com-
paring 'paired reading' with other forms of attention in the context of
reading.

I asked Lynne and her mother to demonstrate their 'paired reading'
to me. They started together, kept good pace, and changed gear to
independent reading without a hitch. Mother's praise was a bit thin
and she tended to say 'no, have another go', when Lynne ran into
trouble, rather than giving her the answer after four seconds of effort.
Lynne knocked quickly, and the gear change back to simultaneous
reading was smooth. Lynne's mother said she knew that her praise was
low — she said that doing it with me listening made her self-conscious.
We closed the session, agreeing that praise must be kept up at home
and stressing that negatives and prolonged fruitless effort should be
avoided. I went home to analyse the tape recording we had made, and
the family went home to continue 'paired reading' each evening.

At our subsequent fortnightly check-up sessions, we made minor amendments to routines again; touches on the controls to keep the technique on track. This adherence to technique may sound dogmatic — but ill-supervised techniques which peter out do not produce results. The 'paired reading' technique appears effective as described but marked variations from it may not be, and one has to hold a technique constant to test its results.

Lynne's reading changed as check sessions progressed. Outside 'paired reading' work, she was reading words on the television screen and advertisement hoardings and had joined the library (apparently her own idea). In 'paired reading', she was showing two effects common after long use of the technique. Firstly, her individual reading had sped up markedly. The only problem with this was that she was now making numerous 'careless' errors — misreading and missings out of small words like 'if', 'to' and 'but'. Ironically, tricky words and long words seemed relatively little problem. This often happens as children's reading improves, with paired reading or otherwise. Difficult words are often distinctive enough to be memorable, while small words are less distinctive and more easily missed. A child whose eyes are on the difficult mountain of a word ahead often trips over the molehills on route. The countermeasure was for her mother to slow Lynne's solo reading pace down, using her finger to control things by pointing to the words as they were to be read. She found she had to take care not to tap the page too hard and so move it, making it hard for Lynne to read.

The second change was the rapidity of Lynne's table-knocking. Far from needing coaxing to knock, now she knocked the moment that she realised she had made a mistake while reading independently. Her knock came before her mother had a chance to give her the problem word — and it kept simultaneous reading down to the barest minimum of help necessary. Lynne's mother was taken by surprise the first time this happened, but now it had become routine. When Lynne changed to a book that was slightly more difficult, the proportion of simultaneous reading increased to adjust to the increased difficulty, but Lynne soon reverted to immediate knocking again.

An interesting side event occurred at the last check session. I had a colleague sitting in on the session and asked Lynne not to knock during one paragraph in order to show my colleague a run of simultaneous reading. However, Lynne could not inhibit voluntarily her immediate knocking. Powerful learning effects were at work — and these were turned on to reading printed words more than on such details of technique. One headteacher commented that you can always tell the experienced 'paired readers' in school because they knock the table whenever they make a mistake in reading!

After 12 weeks, we met for the final session to see whether a standard reading test showed any progress. Again, Lynne's mother waited outside while Lynne and I went through the Neale test. This time I used a different form of the test so that Lynne was reading fresh material. This is standard practice to avoid the danger of simply measuring a 'test practice effect' instead of a real change in reading.

Lynne progressed well through the Neale stories this time — even though she did knock on the table on occasion and showed a slight tendency to minor 'careless' errors. However, she did not get badly stuck until she was well into the test.

When we had finished the test, I totted up Lynne's scores. The moment of truth had arrived. Her scores gave a reading accuracy age of 9 years 4 months and a reading comprehension age of 11 years 6 months. In three months of 'paired reading', she had advanced six months in accuracy and ten months in comprehension. This was excellent, since she had not previously achieved even an average of three months reading progress in three months. Lynne's progress was in line with the average improvements I and others (quite independently) have found with groups of children in preliminary controlled trials. This order of improvement has still been found when a fully independent psychologist (rather than the therapist) has done the reading tests. In addition to her clear improvement in reading, Lynne said she now enjoyed reading, often read for pleasure, and had found 'paired reading' relatively more fun than chore. Many other children have made similar comments. Lynne and her mother left our last session together with the intention to continue 'paired reading' at home.

'Paired reading' is straightforward — formalised common sense if you like — and there is increasing evidence that it improves reading. Most important, it is a tool to be used by parents at home, and is enjoyable to most children. Where it works, 'paired reading' rewards both of the pair — parent and child. Seeing Lynne at the successful end of her three months 'paired reading' course rewarded me, too.

Six

Shirley

A Fear of People

Shirley had already experienced failures of drug and psychiatric treatment before I first saw her. She was a quiet, bright girl of sixteen, whose ambition was to enter secretarial training. For the past three years she had been developing increasing fear in a number of commonplace situations, such as travelling on public transport or going to the shops. At first, she had simply been aware of a general unease, a sense of foreboding. This had developed into physical sensations of faintness and a desperate desire to be anywhere other than where she was, followed by feelings of real panic. 'It sounds stupid', she said, 'but I'm afraid someone might be sick.' She now avoided all difficult situations if she could and would take any opportunity to escape quickly from those she could not avoid. She knew, she told me, that she was getting into a state over things that were perfectly safe and normal, and over a very small likelihood that someone might vomit; things that should not provoke fear or anxiety. As she graphically put it, however, a trip to Woolworth's was much the same as facing a live tiger would be: except that she'd rather risk the tiger than risk someone being ill in Woolworth's. The core of Shirley's life that could continue as normal without avoiding or escaping from other people was getting smaller, she felt she was turning into a hermit, and a crisis was looming with her likely inability to begin secretarial training.

The history of Shirley's problem was totally non-illuminating. Neither she, nor her mother who accompanied her, could remember exactly when it had started, nor whether any particular events might have occurred at about the same time. 'It just seemed to begin, all on its own', was as far as we could get. The history of the problem's development was not much better; 'it just got gradually worse. Not different, just worse'. So much for those neatly traced origins to the problem that other clinicians so often seemed able to produce . . . I had, however, read a report in a journal that had described a phobia as being of 'insidious rather than identifiable onset', so I wrote that on my notes. It sounded better than 'don't know' although it was about as helpful.

If one is honest, much tracing of origins for long standing problems (and much reporting of milestones of children's development) is theoretical reconstruction rather than reliable memory of fact. Where I have been able to check dates in parents' reports, I have often found that two reportedly linked events were actually separated by many intervening months. How many parents of school aged children can reliably report the month at which their children first crawled or were first ill? Yet such information is commonly reported in clinical accounts. Readers with school aged children may care to test the hypothesis themselves with a mini-reliability check. Parents, without conferring, should write down the age to the nearest month, at which each child first sat up, first crawled, first walked, first spoke, and first visited the doctor for an illness, noting the nature of that illness and its treatment. Then they should compare notes.

Shirley's anxiety reactions constituted the behaviour problem in the ABC analysis, and now I needed to identify the triggering antecedent situations. I therefore asked Shirley to describe for me various situations in which she felt anxiety or panic. She described a number of recent occasions in which this had happened; these included a dinner party her parents had given the previous week, the regular bus journey to school, and a shopping trip in a supermarket. Shirley found the conversation with me anxiety-provoking too, as it involved thinking through the unpleasant. Coming to see me was added to the list of events that had caused waves of panic.

My aim was to build up a list of well-defined triggering situations which I would arrange in order of difficulty for later gradual exposure during treatment. However, Shirley was becoming distraught and I did not want our sessions to become too aversive to her or I would lose my capacity to help her. I suggested that she go home and call in again later in the week. In the meantime, I asked her to write for me a set of problem-situation descriptions, each on an index card. I promised her that I would not press her hard when she returned, and that the type of treatment I had in mind would be strictly stressless.

On the Friday of that week, Shirley returned — significantly perhaps without her mother this time. She produced a set of fourteen index cards, each carrying a description of an event or situation that had made her feel anything from gnawing anxiety to a panic in which she had tried to avoid or escape the situation. I asked her to sort the cards into order according to how hard the situations were to face. Fortunately she had little difficulty in doing this.

I asked her if she could now face discussing the cards with me to try to identify the common themes or key 'anxiety triggers'. We had two cups of coffee brought in and set to work, with the cards spread in order on the table. It was not Shirley's favourite activity, but we were able to keep workmanlike and to the task for the next twenty minutes.

The common factor in all fourteen situations, which differentiated these anxiety-provoking scenes from others which caused no problems, was Shirley's fear that someone might become ill or sick while she was with them. Shirley acknowledged that this had rarely happened (although other pupils at school had occasionally been ill or sick), but confirmed that wherever or however it occurred, seeing someone being sick was the worst thing on earth that she could contemplate. The very thought caused her to tremble, her palms to sweat, and her heart to race. Re-checking the past history of the problem, we still could not identify any logical origins for this core of the difficulty. However, we had identified the key antecedent ('A' of the ABC analysis) for Shirley's anxiety reactions. In further armchair detective work, we hit upon another factor which seemed to determine how much a given situation would evoke fear of illness. This was the ease or difficulty with which Shirley could ignore anyone who might become ill, and could make an escape. Supermarket queues were a special problem, because once in the queue with a full trolley, it would be extremely difficult to leave should someone be ill. Shirley's easiest card in the pack of fourteen described passing a woman nursing a baby on a park bench. This evoked anxiety — the baby might vomit — but in a wide open space Shirley could walk away. Significantly, the next, more difficult card described a similar scene but where Shirley knew the mother. Then it would be more difficult to walk away. Her worst card involved being in a lift, stopped between floors, with another person. If that person was ill, there was no way out. Being stuck in the tiny space of a lift alone was, however, far easier; the 'possible illness–no escape' dimension was absent.

Of course, the detective work in identifying features of the scenes that controlled anxiety levels was speculation, but it helped to guide subsequent training in coping with scenes in a controlled sequence of increasing difficulty. A theory about key factors could help later to suggest new scenes of a predictable difficulty for Shirley, should we need more than the fourteen or should we need to fill too large a gap in difficulty between one of the fourteen scenes and the next. It would also help when we wished to set appropriate tasks for her to try to handle in real life. Usually, one has to revise one's views of the key stimuli for anxiety reactions as treatment progresses.

One dangerous feature of Shirley's anxiety was an in-built escalation. Untreated, it was still getting worse in two ways. Firstly, the anxiety was being triggered increasingly by the *anticipation* of a difficult situation. Recently, the thought of going out had begun to evoke anxiety, *in case* she became trapped with other people, *who might* become ill or vomit. Secondly, the anxiety was beginning to be evoked by previously neutral situations or stimuli that had been repeatedly present in difficult situations. A while ago, enclosed rooms were no problem if Shirley was alone in them. Now, however, closed doors had so often been associated with panic at the loss of an escape route from other people that she had begun to feel anxious at any doors being closed, even when alone. Classical conditioning — learning by association — was at work, and Shirley's core phobia was generalising to other things and crippling her enjoyment of life in the process. Learning is sticky.

Now that we had 14 anxiety provoking scenes ranged in a hierarchy of increasing difficulty along our 'danger of illness/difficulty of escape' dimension, we planned to start the treatment process in session three: the aim — to desensitise Shirley to the object of her phobia and to weaken progressively the A to B link in the ABC sequence of events.

Desensitisation is straightforward in concept. It combines two basic ideas. The first idea is that a person can build up a tolerance of the factors triggering the problem, by being reintroduced to them in gradually increasing 'doses'. Each increase is so small a step that one can cope with it, but the end product is an ability to cope with previously intolerable situations. In Shirley's case, the gradually increasing doses of anxiety provocation would come from working through her graded hierarchy of 14 cards. The same idea is to be found in the desensitisation treatment of allergies, in which a patient learns to tolerate very gradually increasing doses of the allergens until sensitivity to previously problematic full exposure is lost. The exercise is one of unlearning by whittling away. Unlearning, like most learning, comes best through small progressive steps.

The second element of desensitisation is the displacement of anxiety by a more pleasant alternative response. The alternative often used is relaxation. One can teach most people to relax deeply, and since one cannot normally be anxious and tense at the same time as being relaxed, relaxation is usually a successful displacer of anxiety. Other effective displacers, responses incompatible with anxiety, include brisk physical activity and eating (one cannot usually eat properly while anxious nor remain very anxious while eating well). One ensures that relaxation 'wins', that is, that it is always the stronger reaction and thus displaces anxiety rather than vice versa (which could be dangerous), by the fact that only small increases in anxiety have to be displaced at each progressive step through the hierarchy.

In ABC terms, Shirley's treatment plan could be drawn as:

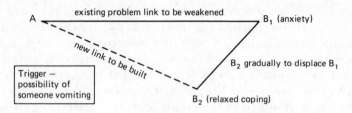

The elements of progressive exposure to reduce sensitivity, and using displacing alternative reactions to excise a problem response, are also used in other treatments in this book (see Chapters 3 and 10). Shirley's treatment, however, illustrates their most classic application — in treating a single phobia.

When Shirley arrived for her third session, we settled down to full relaxation training. The room sported a couch (of sorts) and we began with Shirley making herself comfortable lying on it. The best position was on her back, arms laid by her sides with palms open against the surface of the couch, and head well supported with a cushion so that it would not roll sideways as she relaxed.

Before we started the relaxation routine itself, we arranged a simple means of communicating during deep relaxation. If I needed Shirley to answer a question, or indicate to me that she had completed a set of instructions, I would put the question in such a way that she could answer by lifting her right index finger — a slight movement that would not disrupt her relaxed state. She could speak in an emergency, of course, but that would be more disruptive of relaxation.

After encouraging her to fidget on the couch until she felt really comfortable, I asked Shirley to clench her left fist as tightly as she could and while keeping it clenched, to concentrate on noting the precise points where the muscles felt tight or bordered on the painful. I clenched my own fist at the same time, as I always do when teaching this exercise, so that I could prompt and suggest points of tension to her and also so that I could gauge the degree of discomfort. After a short period of tension, as my own fist began to tremble and feel clear discomfort, I asked her to release the tension, open out her fist and spread the fingers to expel the discomfort, and then let it rest floppy on the couch.

'Let your hand lie still . . . heavy . . . all its weight against the couch . . . Only the couch holding your hand up . . . Feel your hand spread itself out on the couch, heavy . . . comfortable. Notice how those places that were tense are feeling now. Concentrate just on each of those places in turn. They're now warm and comfortable. Just enjoy the difference between a tense, tight hand and a heavy, floppy, relaxed hand. Heavy . . . warm . . . still . . comfortable.'

Then we repeated the exercise, afterwards repeating it twice with the other fist. The object was to teach Shirley to recognise muscular relaxation and to relax muscles at will by contrasting tension and relaxation. Concentrating on tense points is important in relaxation — it is the basic skill in the technique of surveying one's body to identify targets to be relaxed. It also concentrates the mind on sensation, so that one is displacing distracting thoughts or perhaps anxiety with an appreciation of the sensations of relaxation. This is clearly relevant in desensitisation.

After another tension/relaxation practice with each fist, we moved on to other key muscle groups, practising tensing and relaxing by tensing feet up towards shins, clenching teeth, and clenching eyes. We finished by a tension/relaxation exercise involving muscles that Shirley found often became tense when she was stressed — the muscles of her abdomen, which she now practised tensing by pushing against her waistband before relaxing. Most people have some special areas in which they feel tension under stress, and these are well worth including in relaxation training. Throughout the exercises, I kept up the same patter . . . 'Heavy . . . calm . . . relaxed . . .'. One cultivates a calm, confident and soporific voice for relaxation training; the words are important as they can become associated with relaxation to the extent that they can later help evoke it, and can eventually be imagined by the patient as a set of self-control instructions.

Now we turned to developing deeper and more encompassing relaxation. After one more tension/relaxation exercise with her fist, I asked Shirley to carry on relaxing by letting her whole arm become heavy, relaxed, lying heavier and heavier on the couch.

'Let your arm become heavier, lying flat and spread out on the couch. Without the couch it would fall to the floor. Feel its weight. Heavy . . . relaxed. Let its own weight control it. Do not work to hold it up. Calm . . . heavy . . . floppy . . . spread against the couch . . . relaxed.'

With practice, one can test the degree of relaxation in an arm by picking the arm up by the wrist and dropping it back the few inches onto the couch. The hand of a relaxed arm will droop and the arm drop, dead, with gravity. An arm that is only poorly relaxed will have a 'controlled' fall, gently rather than with the desirable dull thud. It is

essential to warn the patient when one is about to perform such a test
— the unexpected can destroy a carefully nurtured state of relaxation.

Shirley's arm still seemed controlled as it fell, so we repeated the
relaxation instructions through from fist tension until this time we
achieved a relaxed, heavy drop. We repeated the exercise with the
other arm, which was soon in the same state. Shirley was progressing
well.

Now I made some precautionary predictions for Shirley. My first
attempts at relaxing a patient had once exploded in embarrassing
failure when the youngster's stomach had started gurgling loudly in a
carefully contrived and supposedly calmingly silent room, with resultant uncontrollable giggles and an ignominious end to the session.
Another relaxation session had collapsed when the telephone rang. I
had learned to guard against such happenings by prior warning. I
warned Shirley that I was expecting her stomach to rumble and that
this was not embarrassing or funny, but normal and a sign of relaxation. I also stressed that if the telephone rang or there was any other
interruption, she was to ignore it while I took any necessary action.

Now Shirley was ready for us to go through each major area of the
body with relaxation instructions. Using the same steady, soporific
instructions we concentrated on relaxing each main muscle group in
turn from head to feet.

'Let your forehead relax. Let any frown smooth out. Let the skin of
your forehead lie heavy . . . spread under its own weight . . . heavy . . .
relaxed . . . no effort to keep any frown or expression at all.'

'Now relax the muscles around your eyes. Let the skin smooth out
under its own weight. Down . . . floppy . . . relaxed. Calm . . . heavy
. . . warm. Let your eyes open, close or flicker as they will. Let all
expression melt away.'

We went on to mouth and jaws, allowing her mouth to fall open — a
little reassurance is usually needed here for the self-conscious who may
worry at adopting the odd, vacant expression of a relaxed face. Next
came cheeks, the face as a whole, then neck.

'Your head is heavy and relaxed. Lying heavy on the couch, against
your cushion. Let it roll if it will. The couch is taking all its weight . . .
do nothing to hold your head's weight yourself. Calm . . . heavy . . .
comfortable . . . relaxed . . .'

We progressed to shoulders, and then each arm in turn. Shoulder,
upper arm, fore-arm, hand and fingers. 'Heavy . . . warm . . . comfortable . . . relaxed.'

With careful warning, I picked up Shirley's right wrist and let her arm fall the few inches back onto the couch. It fell, dead. She was relaxing well.

'Now relax your chest. Let your weight spread down against the couch. Heavy . . . warm . . . calm . . . relaxed . . . melting down onto the couch. After each breath in, let the weight of your chest go completely and let the breath flop out. Relax and flop a little further each time you breathe out.'

Next we went through stomach muscles and buttocks (here one must take care to use the right terminology for the patient), upper legs, lower legs and feet, each leg in turn.

'Let your feet fall away to whatever position their weight takes them. Good.'

'Now go through your body yourself, from head to toes, checking that each area is warm, heavy and relaxed. Melt away any areas of tension that you find. Move this finger when you are relaxed as possible.' I touched her right index finger and then watched it for Shirley's signal. 'Take your own time. No hurry.'

After about two minutes, the finger twitched.

'Good. You are warm . . . comfortable . . . heavy and relaxed. Calm . . . happy. Your fingers and toes feel a little numb or tingling. That's fine. It shows how relaxed you are. I am now going to count, each time you breathe out, up to ten. Let yourself relax a little more each time you let the breath go. The only work you need to do anywhere is to breathe in . . . One . . . two . . . three . . . .'

After ten, I told Shirley to imagine a pleasant scene — a field of corn, shining golden in the sun and rustled by the breeze. I avoided describing my image of the scene too much, rather letting Shirley conjure it up once I had set the subject. As a check on her imagination, but at the expense of some depth of relaxation, I asked her what was beyond the far edge of the field. Struggling a little to summon enough tension to the muscles to speak, Shirley said a grassy bank.

We restored full relaxation and then completed our first full treatment session by working through the first scene in Shirley's 14 scene hierarchy of anxiety-provoking situations. I described the scene on her first index card: walking through a park past a young mother and baby on a bench. I tried to give a definite introduction to the key factors in the scene, both visual and emotional, but then to leave Shirley to recreate in her imagination the scene she had originally in mind when filling in her index cards. It had to be her scene, not mine. Stressing in my introduction the possibility that the baby might bring up milk, but the ease of walking away from this, I asked Shirley to imagine walking towards and past the bench, signalling any anxiety with her finger, and raising her finger twice to let me know when she had finished.

She signalled anxiety after about half a minute. I asked her to switch to imagining the cornfield scene, then followed up with a booster set of relaxation instructions. Relaxation restored, we tried again. A second time she signalled, and the process was repeated.

For the third attempt I altered the scene to make it less worrying — we were seemingly starting too far up the hierarchy of possible scenes and needed a smaller step at first. I asked Shirley to imagine walking across the park on a path which was some yards away from the bench. This she managed without signalling anxiety. After further brief relaxation instructions to dispel any tension created, we successfully repeated the scene and completed the first treatment session. I instructed her quietly — 'In your own time, without any hurry, pull yourself together and sit up.'

Shirley took some time before she could summon the effort to sit up and then swing off the bench. 'Coming to' after deep muscular relaxation can be quite slow — the body, and particularly the limbs, feels very heavy and the level of general muscular tension needed for normal fast movement takes a while to build up once more.

Over the following weeks, twice a week, we continued to progress through Shirley's hierarchy of scenes. At each session, we went through the relaxation procedures, although somewhat faster as Shirley became more able to relax. Then we repeated the last scene we had gone through successfully in the previous session, before tackling the next step in the hierarchy. Occasionally we became stuck and had to invent an intermediate step in the hierarchy where the next scene appeared too big a step for Shirley to handle without anxiety, but we did not (as sometimes happens) have to branch off into any completely new hierarchies. Having a firm idea of the key factors determining the difficulty of scenes, such as the possibility of escaping, was vital to identifying an intermediate scene to slip in as necessary. It was useful always to have such a scene in reserve, since Shirley and I could not easily start discussing possible alternatives during relaxation.

About half way through the 14 scenes, Shirley tried her first real life practice assignment. This *in vivo* task was to travel one stop by bus — a task closely related to a hierarchy scene she had already coped with successfully in imagination. In some cases, such a task is best tried with the therapist present as an anxiety inhibitor, but Shirley wanted to try it on her own. She succeeded, reporting 'nervousness but not real fear', and to seal things in we agreed that she should repeat the task the next weekend. This she achieved.

We progressed further along the hierarchy, now agreeing on weekly 'homework' tasks to be performed in practice. Always selecting a task well within the part of the hierarchy already covered in imagination, we arranged for Shirley to travel increasing distances on public transport (covering enough of a variety to ensure that Shirley's coping was generalised and not becoming tied to specific circumstances), to visit a hospital ward, and to travel alone in a lift.

Sending a desensitisation patient alone on practice tasks like this is rather like a flying instructor sending his student pilot off solo in an aircraft. Like the student pilot, Shirley returned safe, with increased ability to face such situations and feeling reasonably pleased with herself. She felt anxious at times, but less each time. She was beginning to cope.

Not long before Christmas, we reached card 14 on the hierarchy. This was the scene in which she was in a lift stuck between floors, with one other person. With Shirley relaxed as usual, I described the scene and told her to imagine the other person saying that they felt sick. She did not signal anxiety, so after the usual booster instructions, I asked her to imagine the other person actually being sick in front of her. On the second attempt she coped with this without signalling anxiety. Afterwards she told me that she had felt extreme distaste, but not the anxiety and abject panic that she had previously experienced in so many situations. We finished the imagination scenes at this session and finalised arrangements for Shirley to try her final practical test — a coach trip with the school to a Christmas pantomime. For years, Shirley had avoided coach trips; people were more likely to be sick and there was little chance of escape. She had sought treatment in order to be able to face such events and to receive enjoyment from them.

The coach trip went well and Shirley enjoyed the pantomime. The positive of the pantomime infinitely outweighed the negative of any anxiety at people being sick — a vital reversal of previous circumstances, since now naturally available positive consequences at the end of the ABC sequence could reinforce coping rather than avoiding and escaping. Shirley's learning could hopefully 'latch' onto the positive consequences available for normal behaviour, and thus be maintained. We formally concluded treatment sessions and arranged to meet six weeks later for a follow up check and any booster treatment necessary.

Six weeks later, Shirley and I met again. She reported no relapse and said that she had satisfied both our criteria for success: she had neither avoided nor escaped from any situation because of anxiety that some-one might vomit. Although there had been occasions on which she had experienced a degree of anxiety, she had always been able to face these until anxiety had subsided. Furthermore, they were becoming rare and the anxiety was less than before. The trend for her anxiety and its effect on her life to become worse appeared securely reversed. It was now dwindling to the background.

We kept in touch through the usual follow-up letters and the occasional telephone call over the next six months. In April, Shirley, the girl who had a phobia about people being sick, put her hand up to help a classmate who felt sick at school, walked with her to the school toilets, and stayed with her until she felt well enough to return to the class. Her comment was 'I hardly said "yippee", but I did it'.

Seven

Anne

An Inability to Speak

A gliding airfield is a strange place for a little girl. Many people have a number of hobbies, and some have a single hobby that takes virtually all their leisure hours. For some people flying gliders is one such all-consuming hobby — a hobby that, if allowed, becomes particularly greedy of their evenings, weekends and holiday time.

Anne's parents had met on an airfield. Her father had been a flying instructor and her mother, one of his star pupils. They had cut their honeymoon short for a gliding competition week and her father had chosen a job and a house near the airfield. He worked essentially to pay for the family's gliding, and to support the high performance glider they part-owned with a syndicate of like-minded friends.

Anne's mother returned to flying as soon as possible after the child's birth, working for her first 'diamond' — an acknowledgement of advanced gliding achievement. The infant Anne spent her time on the airfield in a carrycot under the watch of the pilots and camp followers who spent their time assisting in the launching and retrieval of aircraft while awaiting their own turn in the air. Anne was fed, changed and watered on the grass behind the launch point during gaps in the flying schedule. In wet or cold weather she was put in the family's mobile caravan parked on the perimeter track, or in a corner of the hanger or clubhouse while the adults worked on gliders or endlessly discussed past or future flights. Anne was a good child; mostly she kept quiet and no one needed to pay her much attention.

As Anne grew older, she sat or toddled on the grass behind the launch point and played with toys. When they let her, she played with some of the older children gathered awaiting a glider ride. Anne learnt not to go near aircraft, tractors or launch cables.

She grew into an odd, withdrawn girl. Most of the other children ignored her; mainly they were boys, who shared their parents' fascination for flight and who urged and itched for the coveted rides. The fascination of flying passed Anne by entirely. She seemed bored on the flat windswept airfield and spent her time reading, doing jigsaws or, as she became older, making coffee and sandwiches for her parents and their friends. Her disinterest disappointed her parents and the contrast grew sharper with a younger brother who was obviously air-minded. She was not rejected exactly, but nor was she a part of the family's life.

There was one particular oddity about Anne, which had remained despite the best efforts of the school for the mildly handicapped which she attended. She hardly ever spoke. She was able to produce words, but limited her entire conversation to single words. Her parents could recall only rare occasions when she had strung two or more words together to make a sentence. This had the effect that people rarely spoke to her. If they did, they tended to tell her something, give her an instruction, or word their sentences in some other way that did not need a spoken reply. Certainly she understood well, and she did what she was asked as often and appropriately as any other child. When really pressed by someone to reply, inevitably she was able to get by with monosyllables. People were used to satisfying themselves with asking Anne questions that could be answered 'yes' or 'no', without further elaboration.

Anne was almost 11 years old when I was asked to help her. Her parents wanted to help her, but found there was little contact or response between their daughter and themselves. They were, however, realistic in their appraisal of this distance, and they accepted their role as the key people in helping Anne to develop her speech.

I was able to observe what Anne did if she was engaged in conversation extending beyond monosyllables. I asked her what she had done at school that day. What happened next was characteristic and I observed it many times subsequently. She looked at me, began to giggle and smile, and then far from speaking, she hopped from one foot to another, laughing until I smiled back — which was impossible not to do. Then she patted my arm and moved away. She had avoided saying anything and I had reinforced her 'clowning act' instead. The moment in which she looked at me before beginning her 'alternative to speech' behaviour reminded me of the anxious moment I always experience before speaking the first word of a lecture to an auditorium full of people; there is a split second when the silent focussed attention of the audience hits one almost bodily. In Anne's case, she followed that anxious moment with her clown routine instead of speech.

It was all too easy to make assumptions about the roots of Anne's trouble. It seemed that she had never been stimulated or reinforced for speech, but instead had been left deprived of attention and the vital reactions of others. There was a failure of her speech to 'take off' in the normal way. Getting no response, people sought none, thus reinforced none. Anne did not learn or progress and thus produced no speech to be reinforced. Her parents' passion for gliding had supplanted the usual set of contacts and responses to their child's utterances that would have built Anne's speech. Yet as a cause of Anne's problem this was all gratuitous speculation, and since it was past history where, by definition, we could not observe or directly test it, it could not be turned into testable prediction in the same way as some hypothesis about the effects of treatment. This inescapable fact was that numerous children have parents who spend little time with them and respond little to them, who nevertheless develop normal speech; gliding airfields are not full of speechless Annes.

The one element in these speculations that we could observe and if required, change, was the absence of 'normal' speech responses. Observably Anne produced few words and fewer sentences and did not respond with speech where speech would have been the predicted response for other children. Also she observably produced a habitual alternative behaviour to speech — giggling and 'clowning' — which was usually followed by adult amusement and adult acceptance as an alternative to speech. Adults (myself included) could be observed reacting to this with smiles and often an affectionate physical contact — a kind of embarrassed indulgence.

Behaviourally, one could form the hypothesis that Anne's giggling and clowning (the B of our ABC model) were avoidance behaviours. They enabled her to avoid speech and they were doubly reinforced by adult approval and by escape from the demand to speak. (Was such a demand anxiety-provoking for Anne?) Furthermore, speech beyond monosyllables was not being produced and was therefore not being reinforced. It was possible that Anne had learned to differentiate monosyllables (which were normally reinforced) from longer words and sentences, and had learned to 'cut off' her speech beyond this point and replace it with the giggling and clowning which elicited consistent and strong reinforcement (and was thus likely to be maintained).

As usual, the behavioural formulation could not be tested directly, but served as an attempt to describe what may be going on by using behavioural concepts such as reinforcement and conditioning. The anxiety hypothesis could, however, form the basis of a treatment strategy aimed at reducing speech-related anxiety, with the testable prediction that this would reduce giggling and clowning. The hypothesis that speech beyond monosyllables was not being reinforced could lead to a treatment involving the elicitation and reinforcement of speech beyond monosyllables, with the testable prediction that multisyllabic speech would increase.

Normally, it would be enough for a therapist if the desired and measurable changes followed the introduction of a treatment. However, this must not be regarded as proof that the treatment directly *caused* the effect. Causation remains a probability rather than a proven fact. Final proof of causation is an unattainable pot of gold at the end of the rainbow of probability — but the therapist can if desired use experimental methods (such as controlled trials) to increase but not to confirm the certainty that causation is present. Most of the 'helping professions' are too quick to assume causation in the work that they do. Behaviourists have to be more cautious than most and they usually draw heavily on statistical calculations to quantify the relative degrees of certainty and chance that what they did caused the effects they observed. However, the risks of jumping to conclusions about what caused what remain high and seductive when analysing treatment data. Usually it is safest to state that what one did was 'associated with' the changes observed, without going further and claiming that what one did also 'caused' those changes.

The ABC analysis for Anne now looked as in Fig. 7. Before finalising a treatment strategy, we arranged an essential conference with the speech therapist she had been visiting to check whether there was any underlying difficulty in forming words. We also checked this point on her records of past medical examinations through the family doctor. These checks confirmed that Anne had no known difficulty in producing the sounds necessary for normal speech. She was an 'elective mute' — that is, she could speak but chose not to. My baseline observations of her speech during visits to the house at this stage supported this 'elective' label, since I had noted some characteristic variations in her use of speech. She used more single words and less giggling and clowning with her brother and other children, and fewest words with adults. People with elective speech problems or speech impediments like a stammer or stutter tend to speak less fluently when facing adults, particularly strange ones, and more fluently when talking to familiar children or to pets.

The treatment strategy that I chose for Anne was the simplest in the book — straight operant reinforcement. Working on the hypothesis that her production of words was a response she could perform, but

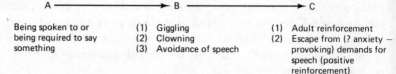

A	→	B	→	C
Being spoken to or being required to say something		(1) Giggling (2) Clowning (3) Avoidance of speech		(1) Adult reinforcement (2) Escape from (? anxiety — provoking) demands for speech (positive reinforcement)

Fig. 7 Initial ABC analysis of Anne's speech avoidance.

needed to perform more, I agreed with her parents to give her appropriate reinforcement for producing words. The testable prediction was that she would speak more words, and the measure was to be a simple word count. The only elaboration of basic reinforcement was that of gradually increasing the number of words that Anne would have to speak in order to earn her reinforcement — known in the jargon as increasing the criterion for reinforcement. We would have to do this to keep Anne progressing from monosyllables to phrases and sentences — otherwise we would simply be reinforcing increased use of single words. Of course, I was assuming that Anne's speech would 'normalise' into normal sentence structure, vocabulary and intonation. In this case, such a 'normal tendency' assumption proved reasonable. That it does not always 'normalise' can be seen in Chapter 9.

Anne's parents agreed that I should begin with regular half-hour sessions with her until I had managed to show some effect of reinforcement on her speech and that then they would join in with regular homework between sessions. A colleague joined me on many of our treatment sessions and also worked with Anne. This had the advantage that any change would not be limited to just one person.

Translating the reinforcement strategy into practical tactics, Anne and I sat down with a 'Ladybird' book. I opened it at one of the pictures and asked her to tell me what she could see in the picture. Although by now she was happy to be with me, all she did was giggle. She said nothing.

We did the same for two sessions, providing a short but clear baseline. She had said nothing. The next session, I told her that I would give her a Smartie for each thing she told me was in the picture. She managed 'dog' and 'tree' and earned two Smarties. At subsequent sessions she named up to five things per picture — but was becoming rather tired of eating Smarties. (Such a phrase tends not to appear in journal articles, where one would talk instead of 'satiation'.) For the next session, we used the same book but I cut out the Smarties. She named nothing. Then I reinstated the Smarties (she was less 'satiated' with them now!), and she produced single words again. Behaviourally, this was impressive; by showing a predicted increase and decrease in words depending on the presence or absence of reinforcement, I was demonstrating good operant control over her speech at the level of single words. I was also increasing the measure of certainty that my manipulations with the Smarties were actually causing the changes in speech. However, Anne's parents were not impressed. Never mind grandiose statements about 'operant control', they commented that it was 'bloody obvious she'll stop playing ball when you stop dishing out

Smarties'. At least we agreed that Smarties did something to her speech.

Having established this much, I then introduced a tally counter. This is a useful pocket device with a button to press and a panel displaying the number of times it has been pressed. Anne and I agreed (with me doing the talking and Anne saying nothing) that she would choose a reward from our special reward tin after each five presses of the button. I pressed the button for each word that she used in describing a picture, and she heard the satisfying click of the counter immediately after each word. Moving on from Smarties (which are such a classic choice that they are almost a caricature of a reinforcer — but most children like them), the reward tin also contained crayons, assorted small sweets, picture cards (Anne had a passion for collecting these), and other small items that she fancied at the time. Dentist friends advise me to develop my work with the inedible reinforcers.

As Anne produced a consistent number (five or more) of single words per picture after the next three sessions, I began to increase the criterion, now she only earned a 'click' on the counter towards a reward if she put two words together, such as 'red door'. Single words no longer counted. So far, so good — Anne made this step up and still managed to keep up almost her original 'click-earning rate'. To check again (perhaps rather unnecessarily now, but I still felt I had to put on a demonstration for her parents). I again cut out the reinforcement — the tally counter and reward tin. Again her speech fell off, although not to zero; learning is not always simply reversible and some sticks, which is just as well since this is the aim of therapy. Her speech returned to its previous level when counter and tin returned. This manoeuvre of reverting to baseline conditions without reinforcement and then return- ing to full treatment is called a 'reversal design', and is often used in suitable cases to test the strength of the link between reinforcement and the target response.

Once Anne was reliably producing two and three word phrases in response to pictures, it was time to generalise her speech production beyond special book-based sessions with my colleague and me. This needed to involve her parents, and after observing our sessions they agreed to follow the lines that we had established.

The reward tin was placed on top of a kitchen cabinet, out of her little brother's reach, and was always to be packed on trips to the airfield. Whenever Anne and a parent were together, whether in the house, behind the glider launch point, or in the caravan, Anne was to be praised verbally every time she spoke, and given something from her reward tin *immediately* if she (1) said anything spontaneously, without being spoken to first, (2) spoke a sentence, (3) stopped giggling or clowning to say something, or (4) said anything at all to a stranger. At my visits, I quizzed the family on whether all this had happened and congratulated (? reinforced) her parents for remembering even when at the airfield. I also spent sessions doing myself what I had asked them to do, to keep a 'model' in mind of what I wanted. As a special check, from time to time I asked the family to tape record half an hour of time when they were all together, such as mealtime, so that we could discuss their use of reinforcement.

The major change of gear to parental use of generalised reinforcement techniques went smoothly in this case. It often doesn't. The only problem was the common one of 'dilution', in which originally tight procedures were (understandably) rather more erratically and occasionally erroneously applied once integrated as an appendix to normal family life.

Anne's production of words continued to increase, both as measured by numbers of words produced in a given set of circumstances and by increased ratio of phrases and sentences to single words. The measures were the family's tapes and the occasional check-up with me.

So far, Anne's treatment seemed to be a classic operant programme with a straightforward learning task, the kind one uses in lectures to illustrate reinforcement at work. However, it was a treatment destined to end not with a bang but a whimper. Anne never became a fully fluent speaker and her manner remained 'odd'. She did however (1) speak more words, (2) use more phrases and sentences, (3) relegate giggling and clowning to the occasional stressful speech situation, and most important of all, (4) continue to improve with time on each of these counts. The formal treatment, and my monitoring of it, faded out with time — but the self-ignition had started, if undramatically. Anne had begun to speak under normal circumstances, albeit clumsily, and thus earn the appropriate response, recognition and reinforcement for this from others. Equally importantly, others now spoke to Anne with near normal expectations of some response. For the first time it became worth asking Anne questions because one got answers. Even if the questions were often about who was next on the flying rota. Her parents were now geared to noticing and responding to her day to day achievements with words, even when the reward tin got lost and forgotten.

On a follow up visit (or was it a treatment-maintenance visit, the two phased into one in this case?), I arranged to discuss progress at school. Anne's teacher reported improved speech. Not very scientific as a measure, I'm afraid, but the question was aimed to discover whether we needed to negotiate a generalisation of treatment to school. The discussion suggested that we did not and yielded the news that Anne had recently addressed her class from the front about a weekend outing and had put up a creditable performance, an everyday event in many a school but the scaling of a vital peak for Anne.

Three weeks later, Anne achieved a summit few normally speaking children ever reach. A radio programme was being made about behavioural work and Anne volunteered to take part. The elective mute broadcast her hard won words in halting but real sentences over the airwaves. Not exactly the accepted measure of treatment progress, but a resounding reinforcer for child, parents and therapists alike.

Eight

James
Faecal Soiling

James was eight years old when I first met him. His mother brought him to the clinic at the request of the family doctor. He was a very scruffy child, with an unbecoming air of 'couldn't care less' about him. Every question seemed to produce a noncommital shrug of his shoulders and he spent most of our first interview playing space games on his electronic watch. I gathered that his teachers hadn't warmed to him much either.

James's difficulty was probably the least attractive problem anyone could have. He would certainly have kept it a closely guarded secret, had it not been so obvious to those around him. As it was, it ensured his constant rejection by children and adults alike. James suffered from encopresis; he regularly soiled his pants with faeces.

Many children with a soiling problem develop a withdrawn and offhand manner. The problem is so degrading and produces such caustic comments from other children (and reactions of distaste from adults, despite the efforts of some not to show it) that such a barrier is not surprising.

Our clinic's specialisation in problems of incontinence meant that a number of children came to us with soiling problems. We had established a routine whereby a record chart for soiled and clean days was automatically sent to parents in such cases immediately after referral, so that on arriving at the first appointment we had a baseline of at least two weeks' records. James had just over three weeks recorded on his chart and all but two days were marked 'S' for soiled.

The first clinic appointment began with the assessment of the problem. James had always soiled himself, his mother simply giving up nappies when he outgrew them. His soiling was frequent, using up two and sometimes three pants per day, and was a combination of semi-liquid faeces and lumps. It was always more than the 'skid marks' that are common with many people. It happened both at home and at school, and James said (with a shrug) that he did not know when it was happening to him. He simply realised that he had become soiled again. His head teacher had warned his parents that he may have to be moved from the school because of it. Occasionally, he had hidden rolled up soiled underpants behind furniture in the house. His faeces were described as smelling particularly offensively.

As the first interview progressed, we tested out a sequence of hypotheses about James's soiling. Some were derived from learning principles, others from the physiology of the bowel — the assessment and treatment of soiling problems needs a medical input.

Firstly, we checked the frequency of the acceptable alternative to soiling — normal defecation on the toilet. James, it was reported, did not visit the toilet to empty his bowel every day, going on average once in three days. This was not always at the same time of day. Clearly, the problem behaviour (soiling) was much more frequent than the desirable alternative — a good indication that we should boost the desirable behaviour. We would require James to visit the toilet to defecate (or at least attempt to defecate) once a day, at a regular time.

Analysing James's behaviour led us next to analyse his response to the stimulus of a full rectum, the usual stimulus for visiting the toilet to defecate. Asking James (between space-invader sessions), we established that he did sometimes feel the need to empty his bowel, but not when he was soiling. His response to such sensations of fullness was, however, highly significant; he invariably ignored them. The only exception, when he would respond by visiting the toilet, was if he (1) had nothing else to occupy his attention at the time, and (2) happened to be near the toilet. Establishing the sequence of events, we learned that the sensation of fullness and 'needing to go' soon passed away if he ignored it. The link between the full rectum stimulus and the response of visiting the toilet was absent. Establishing this link would need to be a target of treatment. James's lack of any regular timing for sensations of fullness was also of concern; he would find bowel management easier if he received the call on a more regular and predictable basis. Some means of developing what the Victorians termed 'regular habits' would undoubtedly be desirable.

Next, we asked whether James actively avoided sitting on the toilet. Surprisingly many children are afraid or nervous about using toilets, particularly strange ones or school ones. They try to ignore the need to go, hope to hold out, and frequently fail to make it. School toilets are often a major disincentive to using the toilet. The seats and floor are often dirty, and many a child has soiled after avoiding sitting on the smears of urine and excrement left by a less fastidious classmate. The doors often do not lock, or can be (and are) peered over or under — some school toilets lack doors altogether. The toilets are the one place in a school rarely supervised by staff and so become the traditional

refuge for smokers and bullies. Many cubicles present the final disincentive — no toilet paper. James claimed never to use the toilets at his
school to empty his bowel, even if he felt the need to go. 'I can't keep
the door shut, so I'm not using them', he declared flatly. Further
questioning elicited the explanation that although the cubicle doors
had bolts, most were out of alignment and would not lock. James could
not reach the door to hold it shut and sit on the toilet at the same time.
So a boy whose dignity and self-esteem were being destroyed by soiling
avoided using the toilets to defecate throughout the school-day, regardless of urgency. The clean and private toilet at home was no problem.

As a further check, James was asked whether emptying his bowel
ever hurt him. (We used his own words for the various aspects of
toileting as experience shows that this is less embarrassing for the child
when being asked intensely personal questions.) Sometimes, a split or
fissure in the anus can cause pain and result in toilet avoidance, or
constipation can make expulsion of faeces hard and painful. No, in
James's case, it did not hurt.

Many people are very concerned at the effects of diet on bowel
control which are likely to be more direct than the various allergy or
food-reaction possibilities often considered in relation to a range of
disorders. Some children eat the most peculiar diets and the extremes
of either laxity or constipation can create obstacles to full and reliable
bowel control. However, James's diet, as described by his parents, did
not strike us as outside normal limits. It included reasonable amounts
of vegetables and therefore fibre. Sometimes James ate bran at breakfast. We often provided families with a preprinted sheet of dietary
advice (colleagues were keen on the control of hyperactivity by exclud-
ing certain chemicals from the diet, and we used to run a special dietary
session at the clinic, so we had some information about 'normal' diets
as well). This seemed unnecessary in James's case, however.

In the ABC format, one is interested in possible reinforcers that may
be maintaining a problem behaviour. Soiling rarely produces obvious
pay offs — it stretches credulity to regard attention or alternatively
'getting back at parents', as big enough pay offs to outweigh the
unpleasant impact of soiling itself on the sufferer. However, there is a
concept known as 'secondary gain', whereby although a particular
problem may be extremely distressing, it nevertheless indirectly serves
a permanent function in the patient's life by ensuring that some more
remote pay off is secured. This is not necessarily deliberate or even
appreciated by the sufferer. Was James's soiling serving some function
in his life — such as ensuring that he was not sent to a boarding school?
Enquiries along these lines drew a blank.

My medical colleague next turned to the more physical aspects of James's difficulties. The medical history revealed nothing particularly illuminating — the only relevant factor was that James had been a bedwetter until the age of six, when he had been cured by an enuresis alarm his parents had bought through an advertisement in the Sunday paper. Many soilers also have, or have had, problems of bladder control.

James was now physically examined by my colleague. He was found to have a hard mass of faeces in his rectum, despite his frequent passage of faeces into his clothing. The mass was large and went back along the tube of the colon (large intestine) which leads into the rectum. The hard enlarged tube could be felt on the front of his abdomen, running down the left hand side. This is an extremely common finding in children who soil.

The nature of the problem, and the first course of action to be taken, were now taking shape. We formulated his situation as follows. James rarely emptied his bowel normally in the toilet in response to the feeling of a full rectum — although the fact that he did so sometimes gave us a desirable behaviour to build on. He had not established any regularity of pattern for defecation, so the need to do so occurred fairly randomly and unpredictably. He had not established a habit of defecation in response to the sensation of a full bowel, firstly because he usually allowed other activities to intervene, and secondly because he avoided unlockable school toilets. He was committing the cardinal sin in bowel control, of persistently ignoring the urge to defecate until the sensation of wanting to go passed away.

The structure of the gut, and so the mechanism and appropriate behaviour pattern for control, is very different from that of the bladder. The bladder normally contains a quantity of urine, accumulating prior to the next urination. Within reason, practising holding on to urine can improve bladder control. Not so with bowel control, where almost the opposite is true. The last part of the gut, the rectum, is normally empty. It is very sensitive to having its walls stretched by the presence of any faeces and this stretching produces the urge to empty in the toilet. In most people, the rectum remains empty most of the day and then fills on a regular cycle shortly before a regular visit to the toilet.

For many soiling children, a vicious circle has taken over instead. If the child for any reason holds on instead of responding to the urge to empty by visiting the toilet, the rectum adjusts to being stretched and the urgency passes away. This may seem a useful disappearance of an inconvenient urge at the time, but the faeces stretching the rectum are still there. If not disposed of, this mass of faeces will soon be joined by more and a retained blockage builds up. Such a mass is increasingly difficult and even painful to get rid of into the toilet. Added to this problem, the now permanently stretched rectum loses its sensitivity so that the child is no longer able to detect the need to defecate. His bowel control has lost its guidance system.

James's habit of ignoring a stretched rectum until the urge passed, coupled with his irregular and relatively infrequent use of the toilet, had probably led to his retention of the mass of faeces that could now be felt on the left side of his abdomen. He had ignored urgency so frequently that when it did occur his body no longer noticed the blockage most of the time. New semi-liquid faeces coming up behind the blockage now leaked around into his underpants — giving the 'overflow' soiling that goes with prolonged retention. Thinking this is diarrhoea, some parents give diarrhoea mixtures at this point, which produces a quantum leap in the severity of the retention and leaves the overflow as before. Most soilers are impacted, not loose. James was fortunate that his parents had not thought of doing this yet.

We now designed a treatment programme for James, and explained it to him with a description of what was going on 'in his tubes'. We had three aims: to clear the existing blockage, to mould his bowel behaviour into a regular cycle of rectal filling and emptying, and to establish a habit of defecation on noticing urgency in order to re-establish his stretch reflex in its rightful role of guiding the bowel control.

James was given an enema to empty his rectum and to give the starting point for building normal bowel control. We then instructed him to take a laxative, senna (Senokot), each night at bedtime, to increase the likelihood and ease of defecation in the morning and to counter the danger of a further retained mass setting in. Only our descriptions of bowel structure and functioning avoided James and his parents reacting open-mouthed to the idea of giving laxatives to a boy who soiled himself every day.

In the morning, every morning, James was to finish his breakfast with a warm drink, wait 15 minutes (timed by the kitchen timer), and then visit the toilet to try to empty his bowel. The waves of peristalsis through his gut, triggered by the warm drink and aided by the long-term effects of the senna, should reach the rectum and make defecation most likely by the end of the 15 minute delay. We also stressed hard that whenever James felt an urge to visit the toilet, he was to go as soon as possible and never to let the feeling pass away. He should 'spot the urge' rather than accept its passing. We had to get him to use the stretch sensation to signal defecation, to build it up and keep the rectum clear, not letting it rust away as before with such disastrous consequences.

James's parents agreed to contact the school to secure him free access to the toilets during class time. We armed him with a personal wad of toilet paper in one pocket and a steel rule in his satchel to help reach and hold the school toilet door shut if necessary. A chart was provided to record both defecations in the toilet and soiling occurrences. As a counter to the occasional hidden underclothes we agreed that a covered bucket of 'Napisan' would be provided at home, and he agreed to make use of it.

At home, James needed much prompting by his parents to follow his toileting routines, and kept forgetting to visit the toilet before urgency passed away. However, his parents did 'keep on' at him and James did say he wanted to follow his routines — mainly, he said, to avoid another enema. He did begin to use the school toilets at times in the second week of treatment, which we saw as a major step forward. He had, however, worked out his own salvation here; he arranged a contract with a classmate to stand guard outside the toilet door and dissuade anyone else from coming near.

We saw James each two weeks, to re-stress his procedures and reiterate that he must respond to fullness. After a month, my medical colleague gave him a second rectal examination. Although James's soiling frequency was little changed, the examination produced the good news that his rectum remained clear of any faecal mass. Therefore, no repeat enema was necessary, and as the physiological basis of his soiling was gone we continued the treatment strategy in the hope that regular voiding would now replace soiling.

At our third clinic session with James, six weeks into treatment, all the indicators pointed in the right direction. He was following routines 'usually', managing to produce in the toilet on average two mornings out of three. He used the school toilets twice in the week and still had a clear rectum. The only problem was that the soiling frequency was as high as ever. This worried me: the success rate of this type of programme for soiling in children is moderate only, and amongst our patients we have found that if we are going to achieve success, we achieve it sooner rather than later. We kept James on his routines and hoped for the translation of the improved functioning of James's system into reduced problems.

Sooner or later, more faeces in the toilet seemed bound to lead to less faeces in the pants. Thankfully for everyone, James's chart began to show a drop in soiling. He was over the hump and now maintained a steady progress. However, we kept him under close surveillance, since it was vital to avoid (or clear if necessary) any new retained mass. It would not take much of a lapse in James's routines to allow a new retention and put all his progress into reverse. Often after a few weeks of relatively simple and undramatic procedures a 'slump stage' appears in treatment, when routines become ragged — forgotten or inappropriately amended from what was intended. We deployed supervision, reminding and monitoring by record charts as our countermeasures to this.

Nine weeks after starting the programme, James was clean. He subsequently stayed clean on follow up. We had kept him (with cajoling where necessary) on the same treatment strategy throughout. This was our clinic's standard initial strategy for soiling.

When he arrived for his final appointment, James knew that he was to be discharged. We stressed that he must continue to maintain, and be responsible for, his own bowel control. Although he could stop taking senna, he should continue permanently to visit the toilet daily shortly after his breakfast drink and to respond with the minimum delay to the sensation of a stretched rectum. Apart from the senna, treatment now phased into normal daily routine for James. Indeed, the treatment had all along been essentially a focussed version of normal toileting behaviour, to produce normal toileting control, ever since the enema cleared the ill-effects of his previous lack of routine.

As he left us, for once James looked well dressed rather than scruffy, and actually talked and smiled rather than playing space games. Successfully treated ex-soilers often seem to gain in self-esteem and sociability all of a sudden — perhaps not surprisingly. The obvious pleasure in the farewell of the successfully treated encopretic is one of the rewards that keeps me a behaviour therapist. James finally departed not with a shrug but a handshake.

Nine

Hugh
Training the Handicapped

Hugh was a mentally handicapped boy of six years of age, with a range of problems arising from his handicap. When the family and I first met, in their house, I started as always by trying to pin the precise areas of concern down as specifically as possible. There were three chief areas of concern, all areas in which Hugh lacked basic skills. He lacked skills in the field of continence; he never urinated or defecated on the toilet, but frequently soiled and wet the nappies he still wore. As an added complication, his parents commented that he was afraid of being lifted onto the toilet, screaming and fighting away whenever this was tried. Secondly, he had severely limited self-help skills — specifically of concern was his inability to dress or undress or to wash himself. However, feeding with a spoon, often an area of concern with handicapped children, was satisfactory if somewhat messy. Finally, his communication skills were very poor; he could be observed to say little other than grunts, to fail on most occasions to respond when spoken to, and rarely to make eye contact with other people. Eye contact is a primary component of day to day communication, and the reader may care to note the way it is used in his or her own communication.

It was important not only to establish the frequency, intensity, nature and duration of these problems, but also to check the nature and degree of Hugh's handicap. Therefore, I made contact with Hugh's medical consultant, who considered that he had a severe mental handicap with some autistic features. He regarded communication skills as key target area for improvement, with continence and self-help skills as having some limited potential for improvement. It is significant that in many cases of mental handicap the handicapped child is often under-achieving and that there is frequently scope for development of skills by painstaking step by step training. However, it must be stressed that a very great deal of sustained effort is necessary to achieve definite but often modest progress. The investment and returns need to be monitored and kept in fair balance. It is all too easy for the enthusiastic behavioural trainer to set off on intricate and effective training programmes which may nevertheless overtax over-pressed parental re-

sources. I have found myself called in to give behavioural training advice
in cases where parents are already at their limits of coping and cannot
take any more work, such as a training programme. One must provide
this kind of input when families can cope with the extra work involved,
not when their chief need is for relief from the load of caring. Behaviour
training costs time and energy.

Hugh's parents were keen to devote time to a training programme —
as a family they were on an even keel at the time and not overly
pressured. The necessary resources seemed available for the task. They
readily designed and maintained their own baseline records of wet and
soiled nappies, descriptions of Hugh's actions during routine dressing
and undressing, and brief observation records of his responses (1) of
eye contact and (2) of making grunts or other sounds when spoken to
directly. All these records showed a bleak picture of almost totally
absent normal responses. As an added test, I tried to take Hugh to the
toilet to observe his reported fearful reaction. Revelation . . . he was
quite happy to be taken to the toilet and sat upon it. To check that this
was not a fluke, his mother tried to take him. Again, there was no
adverse reaction. It is fascinating how key assumptions about likely
behaviour, once established, go untested. It is rather like the genesis of
some superstitions; a very few occasions in which certain events appear
to be linked (like walking under a ladder and subsequent bad luck)
may serve to establish a long-lived but subsequently untested and
unchecked assumption of inevitability.

We decided that we would start Hugh's training programme by an
intensive weekend, in which I would spend all Saturday with the
family, hammering out feasible training routines in practice with Hugh
for them to take over on the Sunday. I would call on the Sunday to
check progress and try to work on any practical problems to emerge.

Applying the ABC model to Hugh's problems was fairly straightforward. The planned treatment sequences were as follows:

Continence

A	B	C
Urge to use toilet	Acceptable urination or defecation in toilet	Reinforce success by food and praise

Dressing/Undressing

A	B	C
Request to put on/take off clothes	Putting on/taking off clothes	Reinforce success by food and praise

Communication

A	B	C
Someone speaks directly to Hugh, using his name	Hugh makes eye contact/grunts	Reinforce by food and praise

The basic treatment concept in each case was that the A–B link was undeveloped, but had the potential to develop even though Hugh rarely produced the relevant behaviours in response to the appropriate triggers. The most appropriate learning principle was to strengthen the A–B link by giving Hugh a reinforcer immediately the desired behaviour occurred.

There is one very clear practical problem to this approach. One cannot reinforce a response which never occurs. We could wait a month of Sundays for Hugh to use the toilet spontaneously, or to dress or undress himself perfectly, so that we could pop him a sweet. One has instead to develop a way of gradually building up the desired skill so that each step forward can be reinforced until the whole complex task has been built up. This is where painstaking detailed work has to come in, both to analyse the task required into small enough steps in the proper sequence, and to produce, assemble together, maintain and generalise the behavioural steps into consistent complex task performance by the child. The whole thing is akin to putting the bricks together that eventually turn into a house.

To appreciate the task of analysing everyday skills into logical sequences of small steps, the reader may care to list in order from memory the precise actions involved in washing one's face, from entering the bathroom wearing one's pyjamas to leaving the bathroom again. Try tape-recording the instructions, then asking someone else to follow the taped instructions *exactly*, with no additions or amendments allowed. If the result reveals embarrassing gaps in the instructions, the task analysis would not be good enough as a basis for training a handicapped child, although it can provide an often hilarious revelation of how much we take for granted in our everyday living skills.

In the field of continence, the agreed target for Hugh was regular use of the toilet; if we could increase urination and defecation in the toilet, particularly if we could teach him to go spontaneously without being told, then 'accidents' should decrease. With an element of realism, we decided to accept that we were unlikely to eliminate accidents altogether. His parents, however, declared that they would be delighted if we could avoid the regular wetting and soiling — which was beginning to affect the furniture and carpets when nappies had come loose — in favour of just a few wet pants.

For self-help skills, we agreed to work on simple dressing and undressing sequences. I observed Hugh's mother dressing and undressing him. Then I tried myself. It was interesting that 'inability to dress' resolved under scrutiny into a few key failures rather than a general inability. Hugh could not manage buttons or zips at all, and tended to start off with items of clothing in the wrong order, the wrong way round, or upside down. He attempted the appropriate actions, but was frustrated by failing to start off correctly. For example, he did attempt to put his feet first into his pants and then pull them up — but became hopelessly tangled (and angry) because he commonly held them upside down and tried to put both feet through the same hole. Starting the right way around appeared no more than a random occurrence. Vitally, however, he was trying to dress and had many of the right actions. Our training task was to teach him the missing actions and to build up the proper sequence. To facilitate this we agreed to keep his clothing to a straightforward and constant style which was easy to manage — pull on vests, T shirts with good sized necks, and slip on shorts without fastenings. It is my experience with dressing training in handicapped children that fastenings are often a stumbling block. Many get stuck on zips or buttons, or cannot keep the right tension on a belt or sandal buckle to undo it or do it up. Such problems can often be much eased by simpler fastening systems such as 'Velcro'. (Elderly people with reduced dexterity in their hands can also cope much better with such fastenings.)

On communications, Hugh was clearly light-years from holding a fluent conversation, yet his lack of response when spoken to was a major factor in reducing his contact with other people. Not surprisingly, his nil responses killed off the overtures of most strangers and family friends. We decided that the response of eye contact, a grunt and hopefully a smile when spoken to, would represent an important first step for Hugh in communicating with others. We did not feel that there was anything 'artificial' in training him in 'friendly response'; all of us learn the elements of social communication customary in our culture by observation and through the reactions of others, and increased human contact was in the family's judgement and mine an asset for Hugh to be secured if we could.

It is interesting to pause at this point and note that Hugh did in fact have a fair behavioural repertoire in his areas of poor skill for us to build upon. He did accept sitting on the toilet, he did help in dressing and undressing, he did perform some dressing actions correctly — like pulling clothing on in the right direction and knowing which part of the body each item was for. And he did verbalise, even if only by fairly random grunting instead of speech. I made the assumption that he could progress further and improve performance in all these areas. This would be tested when progress was observed during training. On our 'programme establishment' Saturday, after the week's baseline recording, I arrived at the family house just after breakfast. Hugh's parents and I began over a cup of coffee by running through basic rules to follow in using reinforcers with Hugh. These were:

1. Reward only small, clearly specified 'bits' of behaviour.
2. Be absolutely clear as to what Hugh must do to achieve his reward — never reversing the effect by rewarding a good (but failed) try, or by giving a reward to make up for a failure.
3. Give the reward immediately it has been earned.
4. When using sweets or food as a reward, always praise Hugh just *before* giving the food — to strengthen the effect of praise by associating it with food. (Incidentally, Hugh was not keen on breakfast cereals, but many mentally handicapped children love pieces of chocolate-flavoured or sugar-coated breakfast cereal. These make excellent reinforcers, since they are not as filling as the more traditional sweets, and do not take as long to eat. Sweets are good reinforcers, but training a child in a sequence of actions is wrecked if one has to keep taking a 'commercial break' while he chews his reinforcer!)
5. Always use small rewards for small steps of achievement, rather than big rewards later on — a little, immediately, and often, makes for efficient learning.
6. If progress ceases, try a different reward; if that fails, try breaking the action down into even smaller steps.
7. Guide Hugh, physically if appropriate, to help him perform the desired action to earn a reward, rewarding him for success regardless of how much guidance was needed. The guidance can always be 'faded out' later as he picks up what to do on his own.
8. Once an action is well established, begin phasing out the rewards by missing out the occasional one, then reducing them from 'every time' to 'infrequent', or by requiring a longer run of correct actions before each reward. As noted in a previous chapter, every-time reinforcement produces efficient learning, but a 'thin schedule' of only occasional reinforcement helps to stabilise what has been learned and maintain it over time.
9. While giving Hugh standard actions to learn and perform, train him in different situations, using all the available people (his mother, father, elder sister, me — and the occasional grandparent, relative or family friend). It was important to generalise Hugh's skills across common family situations — I did not want to end up with him learning a skill that he could only perform in one place with one person.

Armed with our rules of engagement, and coffee over, we set to work.

I started with toileting. This was a complex sequence which never occurred, so could not simply be reinforced. I had to build it up in steps. Two reinforcement tactics seemed useful here. One is termed 'shaping', where instead of waiting for the complete action, you give a reward for every move in the right direction. A complex act can be shaped by rewarding successively close and complete approximations to it — rather like the party game of 'hot and cold' where one shapes someone's actions into finding a hidden article by saying 'warm' or 'hot' as the actions move towards the desired end. The second tactic is 'chaining', which as its name implies is the tactic of teaching (by demonstration, instruction or physical guidance) the first step in a sequence or chain of actions, then reinforcing it and starting on the next step, until the sequence is built up.

My opening strategy with Hugh's toileting was an amalgam of shaping and chaining. He was sitting in an armchair, nappies having been left off so that he was in the standard set of clothes we had selected. I asked him to 'go toilet'. We had chosen this as the standard trigger we wanted him to respond to (the A of the ABC sequence). I had a handful of the reinforcers that we had chosen for this session — raisins, which he loved.

Needless to say, Hugh totally ignored me. Physical guidance to produce the first step in the chain was a failure — he refused to budge off his chair. There was nothing to be gained by simply picking him up. He would then not be producing any of the required responses; it would have been all guidance and no response (or more likely, a response of angry resistance). So I resorted to shaping. I kept an eye on him, and as soon as he left his chair — which he eventually did — I gave him a raisin. Then I moved to the doorway and stood there, while he could see the next raisin in my hand and again said 'go toilet'. What I was doing was (1) reinforcing anything he spontaneously did which took him nearer the toilet, and (2) reissuing the trigger stimulus 'go toilet' to associate it with the start of the desired chain of events.

Hugh followed me as I moved each stage towards the toilet — or rather, he followed the raisins. We moved from the lounge doorway to the hall, then the foot of the stairs, halfway up the stairs, top of the stairs and the landing. I kept to a reinforcement of only one raisin at a time — reinforcement is best little and often, and I did not want him to get fed up with what was on offer before we had reached our target.

When I had given Hugh his raisin outside the bathroom door, I opened the door and stood next to the toilet, a raisin held out in my hand. The next step was tricky, as I wanted to get him to sit on either the toilet or a pot. We opted for the pot which was kept in the bathroom. I gradually guided Hugh down onto the pot, with a couple of raisins to reinforce the actions. We were successful — Hugh was sitting on the pot (at this early stage we were not concerned about removing clothing). Admittedly the behavioural chain had to be fuelled with raisins at frequent intervals, relied at the end on physical guidance, and was not yet triggered by the 'A' of urgency to use the toilet. But we were on the way.

As far as self-help skills were concerned, we agreed to concentrate on coping with dressing and undressing by standardising not only the clothing and fastenings, but also the sequence of actions required. Hugh's mother and I practised this after a coffee break, taking Hugh through the standard dressing/undressing sequences by verbal instructions and by physically guiding his movements, giving generous praise for each successful action, however much aid we had had to give.

This dressing work took us to lunchtime and beyond. The most difficult aspect was agreeing on (and recording for his parents' reference) the precise sequences of actions — the job of task analysis. (If you ever get stuck, it is worth noting that a number of books have been published analysing everyday tasks like dressing and undressing into their component steps for use in behavioural training with the handicapped.) We also needed to work out and practise the precise balance between physically guiding Hugh's movements, and on the other hand leaving him to perform a step on his own. We reinforced steps in either case. If given too much guidance, Hugh would resist and become frustrated. If given not enough guidance, or guidance that was poorly timed, the behaviour chain would break down and he would put an arm or leg in the wrong place. The secret was to give just enough to keep him progressing correctly, but to take every opportunity to phase out the guidance as he learned. One way to phase out guidance is to phase the guiding hand progressively back away from the hands or feet. To guide an arm into a T shirt, first one guided Hugh's hand with one's own. Later the guidance could be drawn back to the elbow, and then later to a reminding touch on the shoulder. The learning efficiency of what we were doing relied upon this kind of logical attention and planning of the minute details of the procedures to keep prompting, guidance and reinforcement all in the right direction along a pre-planned sequence of small steps.

During the afternoon, Mum and Dad both practised the raisin-to-the-potty routine, and by teatime we succeeded in adding part of our undressing sequence to get Hugh sitting on the pot with trousers and pants down. We finished the day by initiating a simple operant strategy for communications. As the first step Hugh would be praised enthusiastically and offered any other convenient reinforcer, whenever either parent noticed him establishing eye contact with one of them. This was to increase the B of eye contact by a reinforcing consequence C. Later we would link this up with the A of being spoken to, and add grunting to give a basic verbal response. The initial aim was simply to boost general eye contact before becoming more selective over the circumstances in which we wanted it. We would never make Hugh a normal conversationalist, but we could give him some acceptable skills to help him socially by a process of developing and adapting what he was capable of. Building basic skills painstakingly from various elements in this way is rather like a behavioural form of plastic surgery.

By the end of Saturday, we had successfully initiated Hugh's training programmes in the three key areas, and both parents had practised and felt confident at the necessary procedures. What we were doing was neither remarkable nor mysterious, but was extremely concentrated. It was also time consuming and energy consuming. I am always aware in such cases that we have a limited time in which to achieve, before the pure commitment becomes untenable. We ended the day with the new undressing sequence as Hugh was put to bed, after what must to him have seemed a most odd day in which, nevertheless, he had been on the receiving end of much affection and acceptable edibles.

On Sunday, Hugh's parents dressed him by the new routines, and as planned prompted and 'shaped' him to the pot each hour. We had agreed that if he produced anything in the pot, he would be reinforced with a slice of 'Mars Bar'. (We also agreed to give his sister 'Mars Bars' at similar intervals — she was staking her claim to as least some of the apparent benefits of therapy! It is, however, a serious point that other children should not be left out as a result of a behavioural programme for one family member.) They also remembered to praise him for eye contact.

When I called in the afternoon, Hugh was being given spoonfuls of fruit salad for eye contact which already was increasing observably. Hourly prompted toileting was occurring without a hitch; the possibility of Hugh objecting to toileting despite reinforcement was not emerging. He had not yet 'produced' in the pot — this was the next step. All was well, but the workload was telling on the family, so we agreed on certain times of the day during which all would concentrate on Hugh. At other times he would have to take second place to other activities, to minimise the impact on overall family life. The procedures were good and the records were good, so I left after arranging a further call later in the week.

*   *   *

Later that week, Hugh had both urinated and defecated in the pot on more than one occasion, and these actions had been reinforced by slices of 'Mars Bar'. Producing in the pot was always likely, as his parents were quite adept at predicting his needs to visit the pot and taking him then in addition to the already frequent hourly potting. However, the 'Mars Bar' would fuel the whole of the chain of events from 'go toilet' to final 'production' in the right place. Dressing and undressing was proceeding well, although still with much guidance, and I could observe plenty of eye contact.

We agreed to keep to all procedures, but gradually to phase out the raisins (and the fruit salad and the dolly mixtures which had by now also been introduced) for the early steps in the chain of movements towards the pot. We would 'chunk' a number of steps together now as the criterion for reinforcement — he would eventually have to get to the bathroom before his raisin. Given the high level of eye contact, communication was to be developed further by differentially reinforcing the eye contact. It was now to be reinforced only when it followed someone speaking to him — to establish the A–B link between the trigger stimulus A of being spoken to and the B behaviour response of eye contact. Having successfully increased eye contact overall, there were now enough occasions in which Hugh made eye contact after being spoken to for these to be reinforced systematically, which had not been the case before.

Over the following month, Hugh's wetting and soiling his clothing reduced as he increasingly urinated and defecated in the pot. Eye contact became his standard response (as observed) to being spoken to — he no longer ignored people. His dressing and undressing was improving, although he still needed supervision and occasional intervention with low levels of physical guidance to avoid and correct attempts to put items on the wrong way round.

His parents had begun to generalise the logical sequencing and shaping and chaining techniques to other skills, such as washing, with some improvements in performance. In dressing, we tried a very pure example of chaining by building the sequence of putting on a tie (of which he was very proud). I started by standing behind him and taking him physically through each step in putting on his tie, leaving him to complete alone the last step of pulling it tight to earn his reinforcer. Then I left him the last two steps, then the last three, as he learned. He was always the one who finished the task, unguided, and he always ended with a reinforcer. Starting building a chain of skill-steps from the end like this, rather than the beginning, is termed 'backward chaining'. Dad had also been applying the ABC analysis to another problem.

Hugh had an unpleasant habit of spitting, and frequently spat again when told off. Dad now suggested that in ABC terms the spitting might be getting reinforced and so maintained by the attention of being told off — at any rate, it was not effective in eliminating the problem. He tried, with some success over the following weeks, to reduce spitting by ignoring it (extinction of a behaviour by removing possible reinforcers following it). It is often useful for parents to have the ABC analysis available as a model and source of ideas for coping with a whole range of problems and skill training efforts.

An interesting new element in the toileting had emerged. Hugh had begun to tear off and play with a piece of toilet paper while sitting on the pot. This had proved an effective enough reinforcer for raisins, dolly mixtures and the other reinforcers to be phased out altogether. He would sometimes go to the pot spontaneously and grab the paper, then urinate, and take his slice of 'Mars Bar' for 'producing'. The paper was a fortuitously natural reinforcer for going to the pot, and thus a useful opportunity for use in maintaining responses. He now sometimes initiated the sequence and urinated at the end of it, without the prompt 'go toilet', showing that the A trigger of urgency to urinate was coming into play. This was exactly what we had hoped for.

One cautionary tale must be told here. Before I left the house on one visit, Hugh climbed onto my lap and grabbed a piece of drawing paper from the coffee table. He immediately urinated copiously, wetting himself and my lap. Clearly I should have analysed more fully the learned association of paper with toileting as well as its reinforcing properties!

With eye contact, we now progressed to reinforcing particularly any combination of eye contact and vocalisation (accepting his usual grunts) after he was spoken to. Again, this went well — he did not ever say much (bar the occasional, rather unclear single word command), but he could now be relied upon to respond positively to the approaches of others. This was maintained even after phasing out the reinforcer altogether, and we generalised it by getting various people to reinforce the response before phasing reinforcers out.

Hugh had achieved his first completely dry and clean week, and his parents and I were congratulating ourselves on our success. We even presented the treatment programme at a meeting of parents and professionals working with the handicapped. Then our complacency was undermined. We had passed the peak of our success with Hugh and he was not to be quite so clean and dry again.

Hugh's mother telephoned me five days after a weekly visit to say that he had begun to wet himself again, and that the frequency was rising rapidly and daily. I visited that evening and checked that no changes in procedures had occurred. They had not. What was happening was that Hugh would start off for the toilet, begin to urinate on the way, but then stop, complete the journey with wet trousers, and finish off in the pot. In fact, this was quite skillful bladder control, albeit totally inappropriate. The problem was that we had a chain of toileting behaviours that ended with an effective reinforcer. The 'leak' on the way when he could not quite hold on one day had been as reinforced as any other link in the chain of events by the 'Mars Bar' at the end, and so was becoming as established a part of the chain as any other. There is no natural guarantee that any behavioural sequence taught to the handicapped will turn out as normal and Hugh's behaviour chain had now acquired a mutation, a rogue extra element.

We tried to eliminate the wetting en route by various means. We tried to reinforce at the pot only when his pants were dry — but already this was too rare an event for this differential reinforcement ploy to effect a rescue. We introduced a mild punisher — saying 'No Hugh' immediately he wet en route, in the hope that we could reduce the unwanted wetting in frequency and if necessary rebuild the desired chain of behaviours without it. This simply reduced his spontaneous initiation of toileting — it was not specific enough and had the effect of discouraging the whole first part of the chain. We did check for dry pants at intervals between pottings and reinforced these, to insure against a spread of inappropriate wettings throughout the day outside the toileting sequence. This at least did not occur, although one cannot be sure how far it was avoided by our preventive measures.

It was all to no avail. Hugh continued to wet slightly en route to the toilet, even after all training ceased. This programme had grown a decided 'wart' — but at its conclusion a number of goals had nevertheless been achieved: Hugh's wetting was now slight, his soiling had almost ceased, and he no longer needed to wear nappies. His use of the pot, both prompted and spontaneous, was frequent. (However, we had gradually increased the space between 'go toilet' prompts from hourly to natural 'breaks' in the day's routine.) He usually responded to speech addressed to him, with eye contact and verbalisation, and he was far easier to dress, undress and wash than before. He now needed 'help with dressing' rather than passively 'being dressed'.

As often happens, the unexpected can limit the best laid of plans, behavioural or otherwise, and there is no guarantee that the situation can always be redeemed. And as often happens in working with the handicapped, progress was real and significant, but not complete and not without heavy input of time and energy.

Ten

Dean

The Control of Temper

Dean was a boy who frightened adults. He was 12 years old and already notorious as a violent character. He had been excluded from more than one school, both primary and secondary, for violent outbursts towards other children and staff alike, and was feared by his parents for what he might do. They were receiving support from child guidance and social services, but so far none of it had changed Dean's behaviour, and as he was about to enter his teens, they were seriously questioning whether they could cope very much longer. Dean was the sort of boy whose reputation always preceded him; before ever meeting the boy himself, inevitably one was told stories of how he had attacked teachers with a chair and of the times he had hurled objects at people across a room. I had, therefore, already been given a daunting image of Dean by the time I met the rather slim and diminutive lad in the school office set aside for our first interview.

Having read files, heard stories, and met both parents and school staff, I now wanted to get to know Dean himself. I was really more concerned with establishing a relationship than analysing behaviour at this early stage. Dean's case was one in which I would need to develop strategies to increase my patient's self-control, and to do that I had to have his reasonable motivation to change, plus his full cooperation with procedures. Therefore at our first meeting, we simply talked, about hobbies mainly — and found some areas of mutual interest without much difficulty. Dean was used to strangers interviewing him by now and had developed an easy conversational manner. I did not steer the discussion around to 'problems' at this session, and left after about an hour of the kind of conversation one could have with virtually any twelve year old.

I followed the session up a few days later by further exploratory work with Dean's parents and another visit to his school (from which he was suspended at the time for attacking his year tutor in class). When I met Dean again, we walked outside and spent some time together looking under the bonnet of my car. He was fascinated by cars, and I explained the workings of my particular engine to him. During this I managed fairly naturally to steer the conversation into a more personal vein and eventually asked him about his suspension from school. He was quite forthcoming and told me that he had one of his 'outbursts'. I invited him to tell me more about these.

'Well — something happens to annoy me. I can't do something, or someone says something, and it just makes me all het up and angry. And sometimes I just lose my temper and hit people and smash things.'

Dean was not able to tell me what sorts of things set all this off (I was fishing for the antecedents A of the ABC analysis as usual). 'It just happens. Sometimes the same thing happens and I don't get het up. Other times I do.'

This agreed with comments from both home and school; adults found Dean unpredictable. They felt that predictable temper was not problematic. However, when tempers were extreme and happened without warning and when one could never tell whether a particular event would trigger a violent outburst or whether it would go unnoticed, things were difficult to tolerate. Living with Dean was described as 'living with a faulty time bomb'. and dealing with him as 'tip toeing amongst eggshells'.

Dean described for me some examples of outbursts and their triggers. One was the occasion when his mother refused to let him put mint sauce on a plate of chips; he had lashed out with fists and feet at both parents while they tried to hold him, for about 20 minutes. This was corroborated by his parents, who added that little seemed to terminate a tantrum once it had begun, other than simply waiting the necessary time for it to blow itself out. Once they had even dragged Dean fully clothed under the shower in the hope of shocking him out of a particularly violent outburst. It hadn't worked.

The vital information I came away with, however, was that always after an outburst, Dean moved into a phase of tearful and apologetic remorse. Discussing this with him at the car, while he turned the starter key for me, he said that he disliked the way that he was and wished that he didn't have such tantrums.

'Would you like me to see if I can think out a way to help you have less tantrums?'

'Yes please. That might make me a nicer boy.'

It is interesting that each time I have worked with a young person to increase self-control, there has been better than expected cooperation and motivation. Each, like Dean, has — when not actually having an outburst—wanted to avoid having them. Between outbursts, Dean was a very ordinary lad — but as always the most extreme occurrences coloured the overall picture. He was an ordinary boy with bouts of violent temper and his reputation was made by the latter. As expected, the mint sauce outburst, even though quoted by Dean himself, was untypically extreme. Outbursts were as often verbal as physically aggressive.

Before my next session with Dean, I culled the necessary baseline information and 'frequency/intensity/nature/duration' data from parents and school. The outbursts were a 'high intensity/low frequency' problem, and so it was necessary to go back a long time and rely heavily on historical estimates for frequency information. Recording current baselines is easier with higher frequency problems. My investigations showed major outbursts occurring on average once per week, involving verbal and physical attacks, and lasting usually in excess of 10 minutes. Tearful remorse and apologies followed in almost all occurrences. Between tantrums were more frequent instances of 'anger', involving excessive verbal abuse, insults, swearing and obscene language. Dean's own statements confirmed this picture, and he also told me that he often became very upset and cried, often alone, because nothing seemed to go right for him. He did not have a very high self-esteem. (I confirmed this with a test of self-esteem, involving sorting various self-descriptive statements into 'like me' and 'not like me' categories.) Checking with the family doctor, this had apparently been seen as a serious and recurrent problem, and at one stage Dean had been prescribed antidepressants.

In behavioural terms, the B behaviour problem of major concern was his outbursts, which had two severities — 'anger' (defined as purely verbal) and 'temper' (defined as involving attacks on things and/or people). Dean could easily identify for himself the precise trigger event (A) for any particular outburst. However, try as I could during assessment and subsequently, I could not identify a category or class of stimulus that triggered outbursts. No particular type of event seemed responsible — back to that unnerving unpredictability about Dean's behaviour. Moreover, I could not identify any discriminative stimuli either — any locations, people or other circumstances which made outbursts more or less likely. The A end of my behavioural analysis remained stubbornly vacant. At the consequences end of the sequence, all I could come up with was that Dean's remorse inevitably drew attention, affection and forgiveness from others. This could well be reinforcing the preceding outbursts, but was in itself seen as a very desirable and appropriate way of recovery to normal relationships after each storm, and was thus not a set of consequences I wished to diminish. If I was going to adjust the 'consequences' end of the sequence, it would better be by reinforcing outburst-free days than by any attempt at reducing the reinforcement component of the normal reconciliation phase.

At out next meeting, Dean and I got down to brass tacks about his problems and what I might do to help. We agreed to work on the three problems that concerned him. These were 'tempers', 'angries' and 'upsets'. We defined tempers as over-reacting to some incident by a loss of control which included hitting someone directly or with an object, or throwing or damaging an object. We agreed that angries were also over-reactions, but ones which involved shouting or abuse but no hitting, throwing or damaging people or objects. Upsets were over-reactions too, but ones in which he cried or felt extremely upset about something. It will be noted that we were already in areas involving less observable behavioural events. Dean was reporting emotional responses and feeling as behaviour, and in all cases we were accepting that a judgement had to be made as to what was 'over-reaction' as opposed to acceptable reaction. The over-reaction element was a common defining theme in Dean's problems.

Dean on this occasion gave me a useful account of what happened when an incident made him 'het up' — which was the run up to the explosion of an outburst. This 'het up' phase was quite recognisable and took a similar form each time. Dean would feel anger welling up inside him, and (thinking about it with me) was aware that he began to clench his fists. His stomach, face and neck would feel tight as the anger increased, and he would feel himself trembling. The feelings of anger then reached the point where he felt he let go of all restraint and often lashed out. Afterwards, his angry feelings would give way to tears and remorse, and the sensations of physical tightness would subside, although the trembling remained. This was a very useful and insightful account of loss of temper, and also gave a useful description of the physical changes that took place, in a set sequence each time.

At the end of this session, I asked Dean to keep a simple diary record, with a T (for temper), A (for angry) or U (for upset) on any day these occurred, and a brief note of what had triggered the incident off. I had asked his parents to keep a record also, using an 'event report card' for each incident. Such a report card is reproduced in Fig. 8, and as can be seen it lends itself to use in analysing behaviour by the ABC model. However in this case, I must admit that throughout Dean was a more consistent and complete record keeper than his parents and often reported incidents they missed (but which they acknowledged when reminded). As a result, I was soon to abandon parental reporting, and to rely almost wholly on Dean's self-reporting.

Date of the problem

Problem behaviour

BEFORE THE PROBLEM BEHAVIOUR STARTED	THE START OF THE PROBLEM BEHAVIOUR	DURING THE PROBLEM BEHAVIOUR	AFTER THE PROBLEM BEHAVIOUR
Where was the child?	What, exactly, triggered off the problem behaviour? (Please name adults or other children involved.)	Exactly, what form did the problem behaviour take?	What do you think caused the problem behaviour to stop?
What was he doing?		How did the adults present react to the problem?	Did anything happen just before the problem behaviour stopped. Please describe.
Which adults was he with?		How did the children present react to the problem?	What exactly did the child do immediately afterwards?
What time was it?	How did the child react: (1) at first? (2) later?	How long did the problem behaviour last?	How did the adults present react when the problem stopped?
		Where was the child during this time?	How did the children present react when the problem stopped?

Fig. 8 Event report.

In Dean, I had a boy with an intermittent and unpredictable break-down in self-control, who openly wanted to change and improve his control. He was also a boy who held a poor image of himself, was easily upset, and spent much time alone crying. Therefore my aim in therapy was to increase his self-control, so that he could practise self-restraint before he was too 'het up' to wish to do so, and thus by his own efforts head off an outburst. Such self-control treatment is a long way from the straightforward 'observable stimulus–observed response' kind of behaviour therapy. The behaviour and the self-use of most treatment procedures by Dean were to be internal, or 'covert', rather than overt and observable — other than when things failed and he actually had an outburst, which would be obvious to everyone. I would have to rely on Dean's own reports to know when outbursts had been headed off — although with time this should be verifiable by a reduced frequency of observed outbursts. Behaviour therapy is sometimes criticised for in-teresting itself only in outwardly observable events, and ignoring inter-nal process of thought or feeling. Self-control treatments are impor-tant, as they do quite specifically concern themselves with the internal. The important point, however, is that the usual ABC behavioural rules apply, despite the greater reliance on self-report for one's records and monitoring. One can influence one's own thoughts and emotions by systematically applying thought or imagined consequences or associa-tions to one's internal thoughts or feelings. I intended to teach Dean to do this for himself.

In addition to self-control training with Dean, I planned to work on his low self-esteem, again by teaching him a countermeasure to feeling sad and upset, for his own use. Here the therapeutic goal was increased feelings of happiness and reduced 'upsets' and tearfulness, as assessed by his own self-reporting — a perfectly valid behavioural goal, to be achieved by training in self-use of an appropriate learning principle strategy.

My next session with Dean was a hard work session in which we began our full range of treatment procedures. From now on, I would work directly and personally with Dean, unlike other children's thera-peutic programmes where I might work primarily with the parents on control measures, having little personal contact with the child.

The first treatment procedure was desensitisation — but this time desensitisation of anger rather than fear or anxiety, to which the technique is more traditionally applied. The intention was to teach Dean a procedure he could initiate himself when he felt himself becom-ing 'het up', without relying on my presence in a formal treatment session. I therefore wished to train Dean to self-desensitise to whatever antecedents there were to outbursts, rather than spending numerous relaxation sessions with him.

I explained that one can control one's seemingly inevitable reactions (like anger and tempers) by deliberately taking pre-planned precautions. We practised an example. I demonstrated an automatic and seemingly unavoidable bodily response by suddenly clapping my hands just in front of Dean's face. Naturally, he blinked and jumped. Even when he expected the clap a second time, he could not voluntarily avoid the blink simply by 'trying not to'.

'Now let us learn to avoid that blink reaction by taking some precautions first. Keep blinking as fast as you can for the next minute. Then we'll try the clap again.'

This time, Dean endured the handclap without blinking.

'So, we've found a precaution against a handclap causing blinking. In this case, it is temporarily tiring yourself of blinking first. Now let's work on a precaution against tempers and angries. Are you game to try?'

'I'm game', said Dean.

The countermeasure to angries and tempers was to be the feeling of relaxation. Just as one cannot be anxious and tense at the same time as being relaxed and calm, so one cannot be angry and tense while relaxed and calm. I asked Dean to lie down on a settee and I taught him deep muscular relaxation, in the same way that I had taught it to Shirley (see Chapter 6). He had already told me that when he was het up, he felt muscular tension in his face, fists and stomach, so we spent some time on tensing and relaxing these muscle groups.

Dean was a good subject, and reported good images of the scene that I asked him to imagine while relaxed — waves lapping the beach at a favourite seaside cove. When I raised his relaxed arm from the settee, it dropped with the appropriate dead weight, and he reported sensations of numbness in fingers and toes while relaxed. When asked to sit up after each session, he clearly took some time to pull himself together again enough to sit up.

All this was very satisfactory — although our four relaxation training sessions were not all plain sailing. He had a tendency to giggle if his stomach rumbled at all, as inevitably it did, after which it took some time to re-establish things (as we have noted before, this reaction is almost endemic when teaching children or adolescents to relax). There were two more serious events destructive of our hard-won state of relaxation. On the first, I had a student psychologist accompanying me, who obviously fell prey to my soporific instructions and rather unhelpfully indulged in a full-bodied yawn at a critical juncture, calling forth a poorly stifled fit of the giggles from a semi-relaxed Dean. At least the student in question had the grace not to fall off his chair.

The second disruption was more serious, as it came from Dean. On our third relaxation training session, he stood up from the settee and shouted at me 'you're bloody trying to hypnotise me!' and ran from the room. Out by the car, I explained that relaxation and hypnosis were two quite different things; I was not going to exploit his possible suggestibility in any way, and he remained in full control. I promised that I would never use any procedure with him that I had not explained fully beforehand. I reminded him how we had discussed the use of relaxed calm to counter feelings of becoming het up and to neutralise them before they erupted in an outburst. We also discussed again and reaffirmed that the object of our work together was to teach Dean a few 'tricks' that he could use on himself as and when he wished (and he could of course choose not to use them if he wanted). The last thing I wanted was to take control away from Dean or to make him reliant on me.

Having achieved the skill of deep relaxation, we moved on to three further steps. Firstly we worked out ways in which Dean could relax specific parts of his body without having to lie on a settee, so that he could do this wherever he was as soon as he began to feel het up and angry at something (and before he became so het up that he could no longer care less and was out of control). We practised tensing and relaxing face, fists and stomach in particular, and concentrating on the sensations in these particular muscle groups. He found it useful to practise his various partial relaxation techniques at the swimming pool — his idea. The water helped, nobody noticed, and he could practise relaxing in a real life situation with all the distractions and potential anger-triggers.

In addition, we took the step of establishing a special trigger word to start relaxation. This was to be the word 'calm', and I used the word 'calm' over and over again as Dean relaxed to condition a relaxation response to the word. I asked him to imagine me saying it whenever he began to relax himself, which he was now doing partially at convenient times during the day, and completely when lying in bed at night. As we progressed, Dean was to say 'calm' secretly and repeatedly to himself, and to relax partially, whenever he was aware of the earliest stages of becoming het up. We discussed the early stages of his build up towards any outburst that was reported (and there were a number, at approximately his baseline frequency, over the first few weeks), so that he could become increasingly aware of the early signs and use his covert 'calm' and partial relaxation in time, while he still wanted to. He practised an 'early warning system' of asking himself whether he was beginning to feel het up, and of checking the level of tension in face, fists and stomach, at critical points during the days between our sessions together.

Now, an outside observer would have noticed little of Dean's covert activity, and only Dean could report on the use or forgetting of these various techniques. However, Dean did report regular 'early warning' checks, he did report successful use of 'calm' and partial relaxation, and he did, equally importantly, report both failures to use his preventive tactics and forgetting to practice as agreed. He told me firmly that he was convinced that the tricks he had learned were helping him to control himself and he was pleased that he had learned them. That seems to me a significant justification.

The other step we took in Dean's desensitisation of anger was to use the antecedent events (A) of each reported outburst during one of our regular desensitisation sessions together, at the same time that he was practising his self-control techniques in day to day life between my visits. This was the nearest that we could get to traditional desensitisation as used with phobias, although the antecedent events could not be classified into any logical hierarchy for use under relaxation. However, at least we were weakening, and countering with a conditioned link to relaxation, the outburst producing capacity of each trigger of an actual outburst. A typical instance was the time that Dean was on a swing in the local park and was being pestered by flies. These frustrated and soon angered him so much that he threw the swing seat hard against the frame and hit out at an adult who protested. In our session a few days later, we ran through each stage in the run up to Dean's outburst, including his own feelings, while he was fully relaxed, signalling any feelings of becoming het up at this rehearsal.

The treatment of Dean was undertaken to help Dean and was not adapted to allow pure evaluation by keeping all its elements separate and in sequence. I cannot, therefore, assess the contribution to Dean's recorded reduction in outbursts of the self-control procedures already described, and of the token system I added to encourage their use. Having taught Dean a *method* of pre-empting outbursts, I added *reinforcement* for successful avoidance or modification of outbursts. (This is rather akin to working with a mentally handicapped child, in which one might train a self-help skill by use of modelling or physical guidance through the steps one has teased out by analysing the desired skill, at the same time as reinforcing each success achieved.)

My second major treatment approach with Dean was therefore a reinforcement strategy, using tokens at the C consequences end of the behavioural sequence to reinforce successful use of his self-control techniques. He saved up his tokens (cut out from cardboard and validated with a signature) towards outings he wanted, and could if he wished exchange any token for a picture tea card, which he was collecting at the time. We agreed between us that I would provide a token for each day on which Dean had no outburst. As part of this contract, he accepted that I could check randomly his self-reports of 'angries' and 'tempers' with his parents if I wished. In fact, he continued to mis-report fewer of them than his parents did. Learning to avoid outbursts was more important to him than the potential to earn tokens by cheating.

Assuming that some outbursts would 'get through' despite our preventive measures, Dean and I agreed to a second line of defence. This was to modify, and reduce the effects of, any outburst that began. This was reliant on direct reinforcement of desired (and agreed) modifications to outbursts rather than on the use of calm or relaxation techniques, and cannot therefore be regarded as self-control. However, it was an important complementary procedure; self-control was aimed at prevention, this token system at remediation.

Dean, his parents and I agreed on four desirable modifications to an outburst. If he had forgone the day's token for having an outburst, then he could earn back a quarter of a token for each modification that he managed to achieve. The four modifications were: not hitting anyone, not throwing or damaging any object, removing himself from the situation, and apologising afterwards (this last was his own contribution to the list). His treatment records showed frequent earning of one or more quarter tokens — a reinforcement pressure to reduce the severity of outbursts and to limit as many as possible of those that occurred to 'angries' rather than 'tempers'. It was both fortunate and worth noting that Dean never exploited the loophole of earning more than four quarter tokens in a day by having more than one 'angry' outburst in the day! Such an unfortunate development would have had the effect of reversing my carefully laid contingencies so that multiple-outburst days would secure more reinforcement than outburst-free days. Had it occurred, however, we would have had to renegotiate the technicalities of the programme to keep it within the spirit that Dean and I had agreed upon.

An important point needed discussion at this stage with Dean's parents. As can often happen, they found it hard to reinforce Dean for modifications to his outbursts, since this meant reinforcing him despite the occurrence of at least 'angry' behaviour. Often it is truly difficult to reinforce as agreed when one really feels that 'he was so difficult in other ways that he didn't deserve any reinforcers'. However, to achieve the planned results of a reinforcement programme, it is vital that the reinforcer be given once the pre-set criterion for it has been met, regardless of what else may have happened. One must guard against dispelling the treatment effect by depriving the child of an earned reinforcer, as a sanction for some other misdemeanour. In Dean's case, the issue was doubly complicated in that it opened the theoretical question of whether reinforcing Dean for modifying an outburst was more effective in strengthening the desired modification, or in adding an element of undesirable reinforcement for the fact that the outburst had occurred in the first place. For Dean, I think there are two replies: firstly, in practice the pay offs did remain greater for no outburst days than for outburst days (both in terms of tokens and social congratulation), and secondly, the net recorded effect of the combined self-control and token programme was a reduction over time in (1) the frequency and (2) the severity and duration of outbursts.

The next major facet of my work with Dean was concentrated upon his 'upsets' and tearful feelings of self-worthlessness. These moods appeared akin to feelings of depression, and were associated with a tendency not to put much effort into going out and actively pursuing hobbies, interests and pleasurable events. Dean always remembered the bad things and the failures, rather than the good things and the achievements. Depression is often characterised by poor registration of the plusses of everyday life, and by what has been described as a 'learned helplessness' at improving one's lot.

The approach with Dean was a simple one, but a tactic I have used with four of five children with low self-esteem, of both sexes and a wide age range. I asked him to keep a written list, to show me at each visit, of things he felt he had done well, and of things that had made him feel happy. The longer the list the better, and I provided verbal and occasionally more tangible reinforcements (including extra tea cards) for good length lists. The object was simply to reinforce Dean for selecting and recalling his positives rather than his negatives. On one occasion he had made a model car from wood scraps and cardboard. As usual he pointed out to me all its weaknesses — but it was better than I could do, and I made a point of driving him to our unit so that my colleagues could appreciate it (and reinforce Dean for handcraft achievement in the process).

Soon Dean became quite expert at listing his plusses for me, and I added a further element by again introducing a self-control procedure. Whenever he began to feel miserable and upset, he was to switch quite deliberately to imagining a happy event we had preselected from his previous list, and if he was successful in aborting tears and changing mood he was to reinforce himself by recording the event on his current list. (Again the reader may notice the theoretical dilemma of deciding what one is actually reinforcing; was the list entry reinforcing mood change, or was the imagining of happy events reinforcing the initial feeling of misery? Behavioural chains do not have neat start and end points, nor are elements invariably classifiable as good or bad. Furthermore as always, the proof of the therapeutic pudding must lie in its recorded eating. Dean did report fewer 'upsets' and more feelings of happiness.) I assessed change in mood (always a difficult target) by three approaches: Dean's own self-report — for which we used regularly a five point scale of 'how happy I feel today'; repeat use of the card sort test of self-esteem (which showed a significant improvement); and the frequency of 'upsets', which reduced.

As the weeks passed, Dean's target behaviour problems changed in the desired direction. 'Tempers', 'angries' and 'upsets' all reduced until we achieved a four week period with none. At this stage, I put Dean onto what he called his 'record breaking' programme. Instead of reinforcing each outburst-free day, we agreed on a larger reinforcer to celebrate each period free of outbursts which was longer than he had achieved before: he won a prize whenever he broke his previous record for a run of outburst-free days. He succeeded in breaking his record on most possible occasions. This tactic is a useful one for low frequency behaviours, because it both thins out the treatment programme automatically and without any risky termination point, and phases painlessly into an appropriately timed follow up.

Not all therapeutic problems turn out to require formulated treatment programmes to resolve them. One difficulty remaining to be resolved was Dean's reintegration into school, from which he had been suspended. To put it bluntly, neither Dean nor school were much enamoured of the other. My aim was to introduce Dean back into class by progressive reinforced stages, as I had done in other school problem cases — initially staying with him in class partly to help overcome his aversion to school and partly to overcome by stages the school's apprehensions towards him. Although I did spend a few hours with him in class over the first week back at school, no elaborate graduated reintroduction proved necessary. He and school accepted each other with no more than the occasional subsequent disciplinary reaction to the occasional, but containable, outburst (primarily of the 'angry' variety).

At this stage all in the garden may have seemed fine, but it proved not to be. The reactions of others to behaviour change is not always as predicted. It is common for professionals working with children to regard aggressive behaviour as healthy in some ways, even if it is something to complain of, and to regard skill at its control and containment as less healthy. One often hears, or reads in professional reports, that it is considered a good thing that a child 'is beginning to show his real feeling' — even if by that it is meant that he has developed the behaviour of aggression towards other children or adults. So it was with Dean. His outbursts were the source of much complaint and gave rise to a general dislike of an otherwise likeable boy, parental fears, and exclusion from school. However, they were described by some who worked with him as a 'natural expression'; while on the other hand, his newly learned (and by him much prized) increased self-control was seen as 'unnatural' and 'unreal'.

People were indeed occasionally unnerved by Dean's self-control, and analysing such incidents revealed that he still lacked skills in socially acceptable ways of achieving his own ends to replace previous (though equally unproductive) over-reactions. His reactions were beginning to be seen as 'sullen' instead of angry, and 'manipulative' instead of aggressive. Dean acknowledged the problem, and we countered it by role-playing the events that had actually led to such comments — first as they had occurred and then as Dean might have played things more acceptably. Sometimes, Dean role-played his own part. At other times I played his part to model strategies for him. We discussed many strategies for many events and discovered the important lesson that turning up the humourous aspect of situations could deflate incipient resentments, and was generally more socially acceptable than either an outburst or a more sullen variety of self-control. This stage of our work was particularly enjoyable. I recall that we had especial fun on one occasion when we had the need to discuss and rehearse various non-sullen, non-outburst, socially acceptable ways of securing the last sausage at breakfast time!

At the end of my involvement with Dean, we had achieved a net recorded success in changing his behaviour, although with the usual mix of success and some elements of failure. He was not *totally* outburst-free, although the frequency was now regarded as acceptable. The main failing was that we had done nothing to reduce the unpredictability of his losses of self-control. Still when he blew up, it was unexpected and triggered by a minor event that one would have expected him to ride relatively easily. This unpredictability led to continued, if reduced, apprehension on the part of those who lived with him or worked with him at school. There also remained the question of which elements of our total treatment package of techniques had been effective. In daily treatment practice, as opposed to carefully designed research with its luxury of isolated variables, one can never be sure of what did what.

Nevertheless, Dean had changed, and with combined self-control, modification of most outbursts, and role-played strategies, he was more accepted. He also felt, as consumer of the therapy, that he had learned to make himself happier and to be more in control of his words and actions. His father summed up much of the goal of all behaviour therapy with children when he said that 'the important thing is that a problem isn't so much of a problem after all when you've worked out a clear way of tackling it'.